The Thames Barrier

The Thames Barrier

STUART GILBERT and RAY HORNER

Thomas Telford Limited
1984

Published by Thomas Telford Ltd, 26—34 Old Street, London EC1P 1JH

The authors have written this book in a private capacity. The statements they have made and the opinions they have expressed do not necessarily reflect the views of Her Majesty's Government or the Greater London Council

Jacket photo by courtesy of the Greater London Council

British Library Cataloguing in Publication Data

Gilbert, S.
  The Thames barrier.
  1. Thames Barrier (London, England)
  2. Flood dams and reservoirs—England
  —Thames, River—Design and construction
  I. Title II. Horner, Raymond
  627'.42 TC464.T4

ISBN 0 7277 0182 7

Typeset by MHL Typesetting Ltd, Coventry
Printed and bound in Great Britain by Redwood Burn Limited, Trowbridge, Wiltshire

Acknowledgements

Acknowledgement is made to friends and colleagues who have helped so freely in supplying information, and particularly to John Holloway for commenting on drafts and suggesting corrections to the manuscript of this book, and to the staff of Thomas Telford Ltd for their efforts.

The authors wish to thank the following for permission to reproduce illustrations in the book: Her Majesty's Controller of Stationery, the Greater London Council, Rendel Palmer & Tritton, Sir Bruce White, Wolfe Barry and Partners, Davy/Cleveland Barrier Consortium, Costain/Tarmac and HBM Barrier Consortium, British Hydromechanics Research Association, Merriman Inc., Avon Rubber PLC, Imperial College of Science and Technology, Sheffield Forgemasters Ltd, the Royal Geographical Society, Hydraulics Research Limited and the Institute of Geological Sciences.

Comparative purchasing power of the pound

Based on consumer prices up to 1970, and thereafter on the Baxter Indices for civil engineering work, given as a percentage of the value of the 1954 pound.

Date	Value of the £	Date	Value of the £
1954	100	1969	57
1955	95	1970	52.4
1956	90	1971	48.6
1957	88	1972	45.1
1958	85	1973	39.1
1959	85	1974	34.3
1960	84	1975	26.3
1961	82	1976	22.5
1962	79	1977	18.7
1963	77	1978	17.0
1964	75	1979	15.3
1965	71	1980	12.2
1966	69	1981	11.0
1967	67	1982	9.9
1968	63		

Conversion table, imperial to metric units

Imperial units	Equivalent metric units	Metric units	Equivalent imperial units
1 in	25.4 mm	100 mm	3.94 in
6 in	152.4 mm	1 m	3.28 ft
1 ft	0.3048 m	5 m	16.40 ft
5 ft	1.524 m	10 m	32.81 ft
10 ft	3.048 m	20 m	65.62 ft
20 ft	6.096 m	31 m	101.7 ft
50 ft	15.24 m	50 m	164.0 ft
100 ft	30.48 m	61 m	200.1 ft
200 ft	60.96 m	100 m	328.1 ft
250 ft	76.20 m	200 m	656.2 ft
500 ft	152.4 m	500 m	1640.4 ft
1000 ft	304.8 m	1000 m	3280.8 ft
1400 ft	426.72 m	2000 m	6561.7 ft
2000 ft	609.6 m		
5000 ft	1524 m		
10 000 ft	3048 m		

Preface

The evolution of London as a major sea port resulted in the development of a considerable area of low-lying land close to the tidal River Thames for industrial and residential purposes. The long-term settlement of south-eastern England, combined with a steady rise in sea levels caused by the melting of the polar ice caps, led to a large area of land with a population of one million being at risk from a major flood disaster.

The solution to the problem, the building of a structure which would be capable of closing off the Thames Estuary and so preventing the sea surging inland to flood the area, seems simple enough in concept.

To bring this project to fruition required nearly 30 years of effort by engineers, administrators, lawyers and politicians. In this book the authors record the problems, hazards and difficulties and the ingenuity and stratagems used to overcome them. Many people contributed to the effort and the final success. Some are mentioned in the text, but inevitably many are not. The contribution of the latter was no less valuable.

This account has been written in the chronological order of the events that took place, and as knowledge of the natural phenomena with which the project was concerned became known. As time passed, and further data were accumulated and research work carried out, additional information became available and the same subject is referred to again. Thus it is hoped that the decisions taken at the various stages will be understood by the reader in the light of the knowledge available at the time, rather than with the benefit of hindsight. The book is intended therefore to be read as a continuous narrative, and the index will enable those seeking specific technical information to find what they require.

Inevitably both imperial and metric units are used in the text since the span of years covered by the project includes the period of the national changeover to the SI system.

Contents

Chapter 1. Historical background to Thames floods   1

Chapter 2. Underlying causes of the flood problem   10

Chapter 3. The disaster that could have happened   17

Chapter 4. Aftermath of the 1953 disaster   23

Chapter 5. The 1965 proposals at Crayfordness   37

Chapter 6. The Bondi Report   41

Chapter 7. Flood precautions   52

Chapter 8. The GLC investigation   57

Chapter 9. Interim protection, final barrier design   77

Chapter 10. The civil engineering contract   93

Chapter 11. Gate and machinery contracts   111

Chapter 12. Other contracts   124

Chapter 13. Flood defences downstream   130

Chapter 14. Barrier operation   134

Chapter 15. The future (RWH)   139

Chapter 16. Conclusions (SKG)   144

Bibliography   151

Appendix 1.   *Designs for the Thames Barrier*   155
Appendix 2.   *Two designs for the Crayfordness site*   157
Appendix 3.   *Members of committees*   164
Appendix 4.   *Thames Barrier contracts*   171
Appendix 5.   *Downriver contracts*   173

Index   177

1

Historical background to Thames floods

Why was it necessary to build the Thames Barrier? Why were one million people living in an area that could be flooded to a considerable depth in a period of less than an hour, an area where so much investment in property, industry and infrastructure was liable to suffer serious temporary or permanent damage? The answer lies in the topography, geology and history of the Thames Estuary and London.

Before the Roman occupation of Britain, the Thames near London was a much smaller river flowing through marshes where London now stands. The water level for most of that time was at about the present mean tide level. No tides came in from the sea, whose mean level was much lower than it is today.

When the Romans came the settlement of *Londinium* developed on the high ground on the north bank of the river (now the square mile of the City of London). As the years went by there were occasional high surge tides as the sea in the outer estuary crept ever higher. The first London Bridge was built, near the site of the present one. As a result, sea-going vessels found it more convenient to unload their cargoes downriver of the bridge, rather than to lower their masts to pass under it. Tidal berths developed on both sides of the river, but there was more space available on the marshes of the south bank. To prevent these areas being flooded by high water levels resulting from high upland flow or surge tides from the sea, flood banks were built. As long as the river had been able to flood over the low-lying ground adjacent to its banks during times of high flow, the silt carried down by the flood water had been deposited as the water spread over the marshes and the flow velocity slackened. The silt slowly but steadily raised the level of marsh, keeping pace (more or less) with the rising river levels. Once a flood bank was built, however, the supply of silt was cut off. This caused the silts and peats of the marsh

1

to dry out and consolidate, lowering the level of the land. Such an effect can be seen all around the coast of Britain, where the reclaimed land on the landward side of a flood bank is often 3 ft or more below the level of the salt-marsh on the seaward side of the bank.

So the flood problem began to evolve. Furthermore, although no regular astronomical tides came in to London, from time to time the sea level rose and flooded the low-lying land. The frequency of these events was increasing; the writing was on the wall.

As far back as 1099 the Anglo-Saxon Chronicle records that 'on the festival of St Martin (early November) the sea flood sprang up to such a

London flooded, what might have been (courtesy of Avon Rubber PLC)

height and did so much harm as no man remembered that it did before. And this was the first day of the new moon'. This was clearly a surge tide of record height, occurring at the beginning of the surge tide season. Canute, whose celebrated demonstration is believed to have been staged near the site of Westminster Abbey, had died 64 years earlier, so no comment from him, but perhaps he should be named as the Father of the Thames Barrier.

The description of this flood is the first of many records of high surge tides causing serious flooding. Stow, in his 'Chronicles of England', wrote:

'In the year 1236 the River Thames, overflowing its banks, caused the marshes all about Woolwich to be all a sea wherein boats and other vessels were carried by the stream, so that besides cattle a great number of inhabitants there were drowned, and in the great Palace of Westminster men did row with wherries in the midst of the Hall. Moreover in the year 1242, the Thames, overflowing the banks about Lamberhithe, drowned houses and fields by the space of six miles, so that in the Great Hall at Westminster men took their horses, because the water ran overall.'

The St Albans chronicler Matthew Paris, recording the 1236 flood, told of 'the most violent wind and damaging floods of sea and rivers' which led to 'drowning of the marshland'. Translated his account reads:

'Then on the morrow of St Martin (12 November) and within the octave of the same there burst in astonishing floods of the sea, by night, suddenly, and a most mighty wind resounded, with great and unusual sea and river floods together, which, especially in maritime places, deprived all ports of ships, tearing away their anchors, drowned a multitude of men, destroyed flocks of sheep and herds of cattle, plucked out trees by the roots, overturned dwellings, dispersed beaches. And the ocean rose flowing with increase (*ascendit pelagus fluctuans cum incremento*) for two days and one night in between, which is unheard of; nor was there, as by usual custom, ebb and flow, the most mightly violence of the contrary winds, as it is said, preventing. Then were seen the unburied bodies of the drowned, lying in sea caves by the sea shore, so that at Wisbeach and in neighbouring townships and so by the sea shore and coast, countless men perished, so that in one township, not populous, about a hundred bodies were committed in one day to mournful burial.'

This account is interesting because the events are typical of surge tides of more modern times such as 1953. The period of early November would

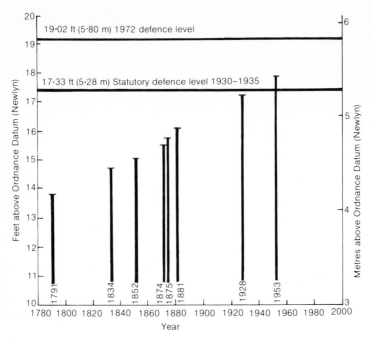

Increasing high-water levels at London Bridge

be one of the spring tides and the wind-generated surge held up over five successive tides.

Pepys in his 'Diary' for 7 December 1663, wrote, 'There was last night the greatest tide that ever was remembered in England to have been in this river, all Whitehall having been drowned.'

In more recent times, exceptional tides have occurred in 1791, 1834, 1852, 1874, 1875 and 1881. The record high level set by 1881 was not exceeded until 1928, when a high surge tide combined with a high flow over Teddington Weir exceeded the 1881 level by a foot. The 1928 level at London Bridge was exceeded in 1953 by a surge tide nine inches higher. Much damage and flooding occurred all down the east coast and 300 people were drowned. This tide caused a far worse disaster in Holland where it was estimated that 3000 people drowned or died of exposure. In 1965 there was a surge tide almost as high as 1953, but there was little flooding in the Thames Estuary as the flood banks had been raised after the 1953 disaster. The flood defences in Central London, however, had not been raised. Water lapped the tops of the walls but there was no serious overflow. Among the parapets most seriously threatened was that defending the Houses of Parliament: this demonstration was not without its effect when Parliament later came to consider the desirability of building a barrier.

In 1978 two tides, on 12 January and 31 December, reproduced very closely the levels reached in 1928—after only 50 years a record tide, the highest ever recorded by a foot, had been reproduced twice in one year.

This record of higher and higher high waters raises two questions. Why should these levels increase by as much as 4 ft in 160 years? And why should North Sea storms raise tide levels in Central London by as much as 14 ft? Before answering these it is appropriate to look at London's history and to consider how the development of London as a sea port, commercial city and administrative centre resulted in 60 square miles of the city, 350 000 dwellings with more than one million people living in them, and the vital central section of the Underground railway system being at risk from flooding of the tidal Thames.

Probably the most important of the many factors in the evolution of the problem was the construction of London Bridge. A bridge, probably a wooden one, was built across the Thames in Roman times. The medieval stone bridge followed in the 12th century. Medieval builders used very short spans for their bridges and built thick piers to support the arches, so London Bridge had narrow openings for the passage of water. In the early days with the lower tidal range this probably did not cause much of a problem, but as the sea crept higher and the tidal range increased, the velocity of the water through the openings increased, resulting in the river bed in the openings being washed away. To prevent the piers being undermined the openings were given floors, called aprons, and the piers themselves were protected by piling. Pressure on space in London, and the number of pedestrians crossing the bridge, gave such an enhanced value to that area for retail trade that the bridge became lined on both sides by shops and houses. The extra load on the bridge seems to have required further widening of the piers, thus further narrowing the waterways. The increased current velocity through the bridge made it a good site for water wheels. These were used among other things for pumping water for the public supply in London, so the bridge was used for hydraulic power long before the days of electricity.

The tidal range above the bridge was therefore reduced which must have had its amenity value. Much of the traffic between Whitehall and the City was by water, prisoners going from the Court of Star Chamber in Westminster to the Tower of London (special entry by boat through the Traitors' Gate for them), or Queen Elizabeth I going from her Palace of Whitehall to Greenwich Palace. Samuel Pepys was almost a commuter by this route. 'Shooting the bridge' must have added excitement to these journeys. The bridge, however, prevented sea-going vessels of any size from passing upriver, so the Port of London developed below it.

In the 18th and 19th centuries the tonnage handled through the Port of London increased rapidly. The advantages of loading and unloading a

Old London Bridge, 1647 (after Holler)

6

ship which floated in a constant water level, instead of lying alongside a tidal wharf and sitting on the mud at low tide, were seen. These advantages were even more apparent as ships increased in size. There was therefore a demand for large areas of docks whose impounded water was kept at a constant level.

In the 19th century Britain did not lack men with great ideas. 'Wider still and wider' referred not only to British imperial prospects but also to the driving spirit behind engineering construction to improve the common lot. Moreover, the opportunities for massive engineering works were great. Finance was freely available and the spectre of galloping inflation had not yet appeared. Impounded dock systems were constructed—St Katharine and London Docks (1805—1858), India and Millwall Docks (1802—1868), Surrey Commercial Docks (1807—1864) and the Royal Docks (1855—1921). A proposal was even made in the 19th century to build a barrage across the Thames with locks for the passage of shipping, so turning the whole of the upper part of the estuary into one large dock. This barrage could have protected London from flooding from surge tides. In the early years of the 20th century a barrage at Gravesend was considered. The proposal was revived in the 1930s when plans were prepared for a barrage with locks across the Thames at Woolwich. The plans were turned down with the approach of the war with Germany, as it was feared that bombing of these locks could close the Port of London.

It was fortunate for another reason that these projects were not carried out, as the complex nature of the movement of silt in the estuary was not understood at the time. The designers probably assumed that increased dredging would keep the ship channels open, and that it was merely a matter of cost. In fact the proposal would have altered the regime of the river drastically, and the resulting siltation would have been so heavy that dredging would not have been practical. The reason lies in the nature of the estuary, which has formed itself into a V or trumpet shape over thousands of years. With this shape it is reasonably stable—shorten the trumpet by chopping off a length from the mouthpiece end and the tides will set to work to adjust to the new situation. The reduced volume of water moving to and fro will not have the power to keep the river silt in suspension, silt will be deposited along the sides of the estuary and the cross section of the waterway will be reduced. This will increase tidal velocities until a stable condition is reached. Reasonably deep water would be maintained in the centre of the channel, but wharves and jetties all along the river would silt up. Dredging costs would be prohibitive.

The 19th century saw rapid development of London as a port and an industrial, commercial and administrative centre. The employment this generated led to a vast increase in population from 958 000 in 1801 to

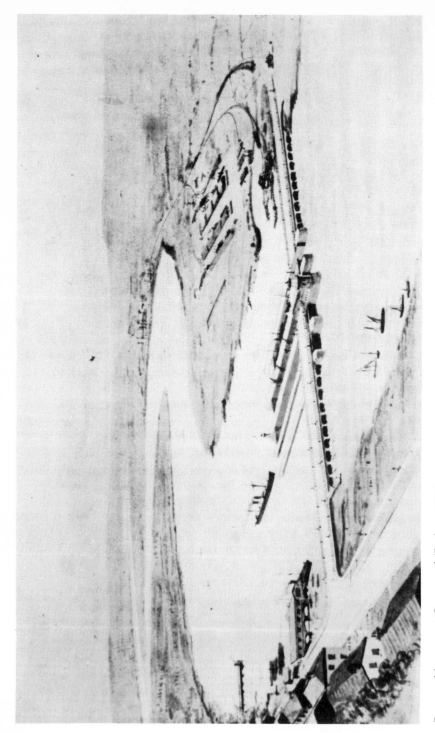

Proposed barrage at Gravesend (Barber, 1907)

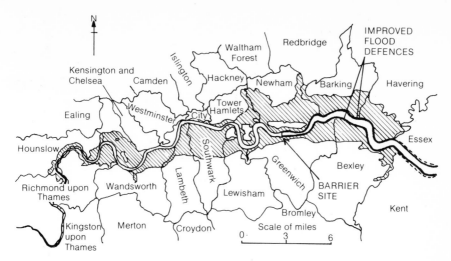

The Thames flood zone in London

1 948 000 by 1841; by the turn of the century it had again doubled. This resulted in an insatiable demand for housing and every scrap of available land was built on, whether liable to sea flood or not. A home on the flood plain could save a mile of the walk to work each day—and the flood might never happen. This situation was therefore the result of normal human activity in a particular setting. The problem of flooding would not have been too serious but for the steady rise in the water levels of the tidal Thames.

2

Underlying causes of the flood problem

As already discussed, the development of London had resulted in a large area of low-lying land close to the tidal Thames becoming a densely built-up industrial and residential area. This area became liable to catastrophic flooding because the land was sinking compared with the sea level, while there were, at rare intervals, abnormally high sea levels due to freak meteorological conditions. Before considering the ways of combating this flood risk, these two phenomena should be examined.

It is accepted that high-water levels in the Thames in Central London were much lower in Roman times than today. River walls and wharves built then were 15 ft lower than those built in recent years. It is generally accepted that some rise in the sea level has occurred over the past 2000 years, but not of this magnitude: therefore the land must have sunk. In 1971 a two-day conference was held at the Royal Society to discuss this matter. It was agreed that sea levels were rising relative to land at about the rate of a foot a century, but there was no agreement on the proportion which was due to the rise in sea level and that which was due to the sinkage of land. In summing up at the end of the conference, the chairman expressed the opinion that about half was due to the rise in sea level and the other half to the sinkage of land. Further investigation of this question would be of scientific interest, but for engineering and economic purposes it seems sufficient to accept that conclusion. The rise in sea level since the last ice age, due to the melting of polar ice caps, which have receded from Potters Bar to northern Greenland, appears a fairly reasonable assumption. The concept that the south of England is slowly sinking requires some further explanation.

The theories of continental drift and tectonic plates which are now at long last accepted provide such an explanation. The tectonic plate on which the British Isles rests had its northern section depressed by a heavy

10

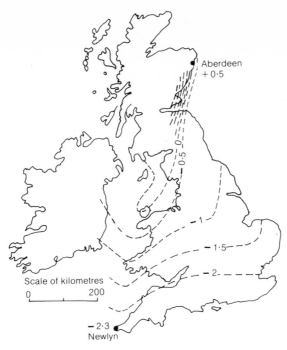

Aberdeen
+ 0·5

0·5

1

1·5

2

Scale of kilometres
0   200

− 2·3
Newlyn

Land settlement relative to mean sea level, millimetres
per year (after Valentin)

load of ice during the last ice age. Relieved of this load when the ice melted, the northern part of Britain is now rising, and the southern part is going down. In general terms, the axis about which the country tilts is on a line from the Severn to the Tyne. This movement has affected the Thames, which is an old river and which eroded its valley long ago. Before the sea rose, and the North Sea was formed, the Thames ran east to become a tributary of the Rhine. As the area was composed entirely of soft materials—beds of gravel, clay and chalk—it was a wide valley. When the land sank and tides began to flow in and out of the river mouth, working against easily eroded material, they transformed the river mouth into a wide estuary.

Sinkage due to tectonic movement has affected many coastlines but in different ways. Where the materials are hard, the shapes of the hills and valleys were not altered by the tide and beautiful sea inlets developed, for example, the Norwegian fiords, the Scottish sea lochs and the great sea inlets of British Columbia. Where the materials were soft erosion occurred: river deltas with many channels were formed; where offshore currents removed the silt, estuaries with wide mouths were formed which became steadily narrower upstream, such as is seen in the Thames, the Seine and the Elbe. As the land sinks, the water in an

11

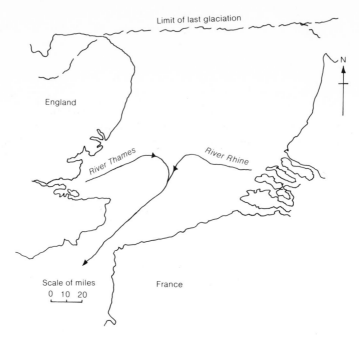

Courses of Rhine and Thames in the last ice age

estuary becomes deeper and the tides, having less obstruction, move faster and scour deeper, increasing the tidal range. As the estuary is scoured deeper the tide becomes yet faster; and so the process is self-multiplying.

Fortunately for the Thames, nature has provided an opposing factor. The Thames Estuary, and the area of shallow sea outside it, contains vast quantities of silt resulting from the erosion of the east coast of England by wave and tidal action. This silt is eroded and deposited in a way which tends to check any excessive deepening of the estuary. The deepening process therefore proceeds slowly. Fortunately for London as a sea port, the sea currents at the river mouth have prevented the deposition of silt from forming a delta (or perhaps more accurately have allowed the formation of a curious submerged delta off the river's mouth).

The fresh-water flow is a further factor affecting the movement of silt in an estuary. Even in a channel with fairly strong currents, sea water, being heavier than freshwater, does not at once mix with it, and the two tend to flow in separate layers, the salt water below the fresh. One of the first examples of this to be widely known was during the First World War, when British submarines went through the Dardanelles. The rivers flowing into the Black Sea (the Danube, Dnieper, Don and others) cause an outward fresh-water flow through the straits. This passes over the salt

12

water, the two not mixing over a considerable area. A submarine trimmed to navigate in one layer was suddenly in difficulties when it met the other.

There are similar phenomena at the Straits of Gibraltar and at the mouth of the River Amazon, where the fresh-water flow of the river floats over the salt sea water for 100 miles into the Atlantic Ocean. This phenomenon complicates the movement of silt in an estuary still further.

Satisfactory predictions, based on mathematical calculations as to how the various arrangements for the barrier would affect the silt's movement, could not be made and large and expensive physical hydraulic models had to be built.

Additional sinkage in the centre of London has been caused by the extraction of water. London sits on a geological basin covered by a thick clay lid. Below this clay lie gravels, sands and the chalk. Rain falls on the high ground forming the rim of this basin: in the north the Chilterns, northern Essex and Hertfordshire; in the south the North Downs. The rain then percolates down into the centre of the basin. In the 19th century many owners of factories and buildings found that it was cheaper to drill down through the clay and tap this source of water than to buy it from the then water companies. There are 350 of these boreholes. Through overpumping, the water levels in wells in London, which were generally 6–9 m below Ordnance Datum (approximately mean sea level) in 1845, had fallen to 60–90 m below OD (75 m under the area around St Paul's) by 1936. Since that time there has been a modest recovery, as a result of reduced abstraction. The resultant drying-out of the clay and the chalk caused shrinkage and this in turn caused settlement; in the area of St Paul's this is estimated at 0.2 m. This may not seem much, but a great deal more water comes over a flood wall over-topped by 0.5 m than 0.3 m, due not only to the greater depth, but also to the longer period of time that the tide level is higher than the crest of the wall. London is not alone with this problem. In Venice, the settlement caused by overpumping of ground water has been much more serious, and the Government has now prohibited the pumping of groundwater in this area.

The total effect of all these factors—the rise in sea level, the settlement of south-east England, the higher rate of settlement in London itself, and the increase in the tidal range in the Thames Estuary—has led to an observed rise in high waters at London Bridge of about 0.8 m per century. However, this steady rise is not the main cause of London's floods—it merely aggravates the problem. The rise is predictable and could be contained by raising the flood defence banks; flooding would initially be quite minor. It is the sea flood, when the North Sea surge many feet high overtops the flood defences, that presents the main

13

problem and risk of catastrophe.

Surge tides in the North Sea have their genesis off the coast of Canada in the region of the Newfoundland Banks. Areas of low atmospheric pressure, or depressions, arise as a result of the meeting of the warm Gulf Stream and the cold Labrador Current off the Labrador coast. Cyclonic winds are generated around the centres of these depressions and, as a result of the wind patterns in the Northern Hemisphere, these depressions move eastwards across the Atlantic towards Europe. Atmospheric pressure affects the level of the sea: high pressure depresses the surface and low pressure raises it. Beneath the depression a hump of water forms, only about a foot high but a thousand miles in diameter and moving perhaps at 40 or 50 miles per hour. Many million tons of water moving at this speed represent an enormous amount of energy and the dynamic effect of the eastward movement magnifies the height of the hump, which is further increased as it moves from the deep waters of the Atlantic into the shallower waters of the continental shelf.

Usually these depressions move north-east between Iceland and Scandinavia and do little harm. Occasionally, and unpredictably, they turn

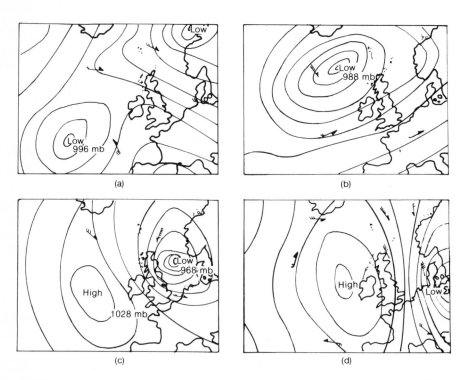

Weather map showing development of storm surge (courtesy of the Royal Geographical Society, from Geog. J., *1979,* **145**, *2, 247)*

east and pass across northern Germany. This brings the hump of water into the northern North Sea. If the depression is a deep one with high pressure to the west, then very strong northerly gales will blow on the flank of the depression, and the hump of water is driven south into the funnel formed by the converging coastlines of England and the Continent. This amplifies the hump, which is further increased by the drag of the wind on the surface of the sea. As the water moves south the rotation of the earth throws the water against the east coast of England, following the pattern of movement of the astronomical tide. The Straits of Dover are too narrow and shallow to allow the large volume of water to pass through. The speed of movement of the depression and the period of time over which the strong northerly gales continue to blow now become important factors. If the high wind strength continues in the same area as high water of the normal predicted tide, then the level of high water will be much increased.

If the normal predicted tide is by chance a high spring tide produced by the combined gravitational forces of sun and moon, then the situation becomes very serious. The combination of all these factors is fortunately a rare event, but still inevitable. Past surges have raised the high-water level at Southend by as much as 8½ ft, and by 14 ft on the rising tide, but surges considerably higher than these are thought possible in the future.

The reader may think that the power of the wind has been overestimated, but the effect on a water surface can be seen by watching it blow over a puddle. At first the surface is roughened, then the wind gets hold of the crests of the little waves and pushes the water along. The effect on larger bodies is the same.

A simple account has been given of the 'hump' moving across the Atlantic. There is, however, an added complication. The inertia of the water and, where there is a confined space, the friction of the water against the bottom of the sea or estuary, delays the water's response to atmospheric changes and this delay generally persists until the atmospheric pressure has changed again. In other words, there is a 'damping action' so that excessive surges tend to fade. Unfortunately this does not always occur. The build-up of energy by the travelling hump in the open sea can be compared with the build-up of energy in front of an aeroplane flying at the speed of sound, which creates a sonic bang. Observations of water humps as they travel round the north of Scotland at Lerwick and Stornoway have shown that a hump travelling in a sea where the waves are long can be multiplied in height up to eight times; but in a sea where the waves are short the height of the hump can be multiplied up to 25 times. A very modest hump, perhaps reflected by a drop of an inch of mercury in the barometer, can be magnified by this movement into a disastrous 8 ft or 10 ft of tidal height.

The normal tide moves in from the Atlantic and down the east coast in the form of a long wave, the wave length being about 500 miles and the cyclic time 11 hours 40 minutes. The rate of movement of this wave is not constant but, as explained above, depends on the depth of the sea and the shape of the coastline. It takes about 12 hours for the tide to move from the north of Scotland to the Thames Estuary.

So far we have only been concerned with surge tides in the open sea, the problem as it is outside the Thames Estuary, and as recorded on the tide gauge at Southend. Surge tides, however, become more serious at points higher up the estuary. When a wave enters a V-shaped or trumpet-shaped estuary, its height will build up as it reaches the narrower part. This common-sense observation can be explained in scientific terms. The wave enters the estuary with a certain quantity of energy. This is distributed over a large body of water occupying the full width. As the wave moves up the estuary, the same amount of energy, less some lost by friction and other causes, is passed into the smaller body of water in the narrower parts, so that the height increases. Losses due to friction against the bottom part of the estuary will obviously be decreased if the tide is given a deep channel instead of running over shallows. Losses caused by irregularities in the sides of the estuaries, pro-jections, bays and so on, which cause swirls, will obviously be less if the sides have been straightened out. Over the years the flow of the tide in the Thames has been eased in both of these ways: the sides, formerly marshlands, have been tidied up and straightened out by flood banks (e.g. the Victoria and Albert Embankments in Central London), and the smooth bank lines have increased the velocity of the tidal current which has in turn helped to scour out the main channel to a greater depth. The passage of ships, with their propellers violently agitating the water near the bottom and so churning up the mud, has also increased the depth. In other estuaries dredging performs all or part of this task, but the Thames is fortunate in that very little dredging of the main channel has been necessary. This self-maintaining quality of the estuary has been of great benefit to London, but efforts to preserve it caused many difficulties and obstructed progress with the Thames Barrier project.

As a result of the shape of the Thames Estuary a spring tide, which occurs every fortnight, when the gravitational forces of sun and moon work together, will normally reach a level at London Bridge which is a metre higher than the level reached at Southend on the same tide.

3

The disaster that could have happened

The 1953 surge tide rose only 3.7 ft above the high-water level of a high spring tide at London Bridge. This was sufficient to overtop and breach flood defences all down the east coast of England. Some 160 000 acres of farm land were flooded, together with 24 000 houses, 200 major industrial premises, 200 miles of railway, twelve gasworks and two large electricity generating stations. Over 300 people were drowned, from invalids in their beds to engineers inspecting flood defences at the height of the storm, as well as 11 000 cattle, 9000 sheep, 2400 pigs, 34 000 poultry and 70 horses. Over 100 000 tons of gypsum were required to restore the land that had been affected by salt. The cost of this disaster would have been measured in thousands of millions of pounds at today's prices. The 1962 surge tide at Hamburg rose 14 ft above the predicted tide. The 1953 tide lapped the tops of the parapet walls in Central London: obviously a surge very much less than that at Hamburg could do great damage.

A small overtopping for half an hour would merely flood the riverside streets. Even this might have serious consequences for the great riverside buildings; and comparatively small quantities of water entering the Underground at the riverside stations could have disastrous consequences. A surge of 6 ft above the 1953 flood tide (the possibility considered by the Thames Technical Panel, see p. 28) would flood wide and exceedingly important areas. All buildings in the area would have their basements flooded and, depending on their position, up to 10 ft of water above the ground floors. Buildings outside the area would have their basements flooded by flood water backing up along the drains. A surge only 2 ft higher than that of 1953 would flood the greater part of the area if the high-tide level persisted long enough for sufficient water to pass over the walls. In this connection the engineers responsible for the river walls believed that if they were overtopped by, say, a couple of feet, the pressure would be sufficient to destroy parts of the wall so that additional volumes of water could pour through the gaps.

Estimation of the quantity of water which would pass over the flood walls due to surges of different height and duration is a complex matter. First, owing to raising of the Kent and Essex flood banks below London, a surge which had the same height at Southend as that of 1953 would produce higher levels at London Bridge because there would, today, be no overflow or loss through breaches in the banks downriver of London. However, a surge 6 ft higher than that in 1953 at Southend would be relieved as soon as it started to overflow the downriver banks, and flood levels in London's streets would depend on the duration of the surge and on the extent to which walls might be damaged. Reduction of flood level due to overflows in downriver areas would diminish or eventually cease, if the surge were prolonged, as the areas into which overflow was possible became full of water.

The Underground would be affected to a greater extent than any other organisation. It would be hit to the maximum extent by a comparatively small overflow. After careful consideration London Transport found that it would be impracticable to provide and operate flood stops at all the points where water could enter the Underground railway system, such as open tunnel mouths where the railways come to the surface, station entrances, ventilating shafts and the huge rolling-stock lift at Waterloo. The watertight doors installed as a wartime precaution in some of the tunnels are so placed that they would stop water which had entered an under-river tunnel through a bomb crater in the river bed from passing farther from the river than the door; they would not stop water which had entered the riverside Underground stations from flooding the tunnels running away from the river banks. Such flooding would put the system out of action between Hammersmith, Stratford, Kings Cross and Clapham. After extensive flooding a limited service might be restarted in a month or so, perhaps with many escalators and much of the signalling out of use. Full recovery might take a year.

There would be vast damage and interference with business. Streets would rapidly be flooded and rendered impassable: after a few hours the water would slowly drain back towards the river, and pass into the surface water drains. Drainage should be fairly rapid during low-tide periods, but a good deal of the area which would be flooded is below the level of spring tides, so that for part of the tide cycle the rate of drainage would be reduced. Drainage through the foul water sewers would be slow, as their capacity is small compared with the volume of water to be drained away. The Greater London Council's surface water pumping stations are in general above flood level or have flood protection. They

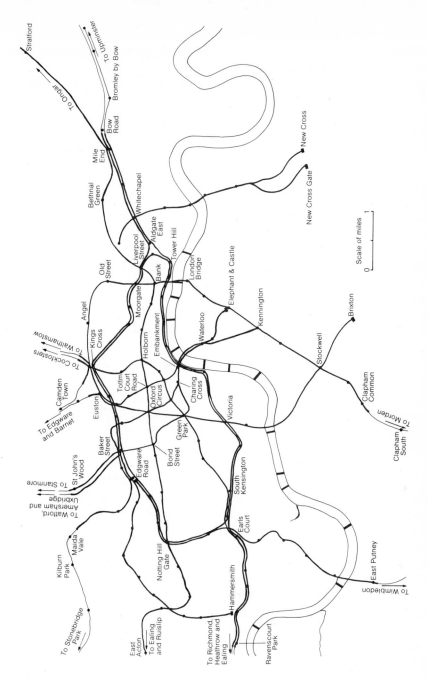

London Underground railway system; possible extent of flooding by storm surge (marked by lines in bold)

would be able to operate and therefore the flood water in the streets should all be drained away after a few days.

A surge tide would cause strong currents in the river and would pick up a great deal of mud. This would be deposited in the areas flooded. All basements in the flooded area would be full of water. Some have connections to the sewers or drains; water would slowly drain away from those. Other basements, however, have no such connections and would have to await pumping out by the fire brigade or other arrangements. This problem would be so great that it would be necessary for the London Fire Brigade to obtain the help of other brigades. Some of the basements would have been flooded by back-flow from the sewers; this back-flow would carry and deposit solid pollution.

It is not probable that there would be serious interference with water supplies. Gas supplies might be affected by flooding of the riverside gasworks. Electricity supplies might be affected by flood water at the riverside generating stations, but trouble here might be ameliorated by supplies from outside through the national grid; there would, however, be extensive interference with distribution owing to flooding of substations. The underground telephone cables should not suffer badly. The system is, however, powered by massive 50 V accumulators, normally housed low down, at each exchange. Many of these might well be ruined by flooding.

Many of the great riverside buildings would be badly affected. The Houses of Parliament have much accommodation at a low level. County Hall has its telephone exchange in the basement. The Ministry of Defence and Shell buildings each have four or five storeys below ground. At Somerset House large volumes of important records were in the basement. At the Tate Gallery part of the permanent collection would be flooded, together with a great many paintings in storage; any curiosities on the main floor are above flood level. (After the 1928 floods the Turner drawings and water colours were taken to the British Museum.) In the docks the bulk of the storage is at ground level; this would all be flooded. Suitable attention to lines, springs and fenders should, however, prevent damage to moored vessels. Unattended small craft might finish high and dry.

After the flood water had drained away a vast amount of cleaning and drying would be necessary before basements and ground floors were usable again. The upper floors could of course continue in use, subject to short-term difficulties with electricity supplies and probable fairly prolonged trouble with telephones.

The floodable area contains a population of 1.2 million in 350 000 dwellings. About a million and a half people work in it. This is equivalent to a town larger than Birmingham.

The only flooding of a great city by a surge tide with which the possible events in London can conveniently be compared was the flooding of part of Hamburg in 1962. Apart from the absence of important public buildings, the area flooded in Hamburg contained a similar mixed residential and commercial development to that which might be flooded in London. There were 120 000 people in the flooded area of whom 34 000 were directly affected; 20 000 had to be temporarily evacuated and 5000 provided with new dwellings. There were 312 dead (but mostly outside the city). The floodable area in London is 75 square miles (comparable with the 79 square miles of Birmingham). The area flooded in Hamburg was 1.7 square miles; the sum paid out for damage claims to goods and property (excluding the port) was the equivalent of £16 million at 1966 prices. On this basis the equivalent for household, office and shop damage in London would have been £700 million (at 1966 values). Dependence can be placed on the accuracy of the Hamburg records of the cost of the flood damage—with typical German thoroughness a corps of assessors was employed and every claim investigated on the spot.

Some indication of damage which might be incurred in the Port of London can be obtained by considering the amount of merchandise which would be at risk. In 1966 the annual value of traffic passing through was of the order of £3000 million. That part of it which might be damaged by flooding is what would be on the quays and the ground floors of transit sheds and warehouses at any one time (excluding the Tilbury Docks). This might be of the order of £10 million. Some of this cargo, steel sections and so on, might not suffer damage. Timber would float and could be partially recoverable. However, the bulk of the cargo in London is manufactured goods—food, etc.—which would be badly damaged by immersion. Interruption of working during the flooding and sorting out the mess afterwards would inevitably deprive the port of many days' effective working. This would hold up shipping and incoming loaded railway rolling stock and lorries. Massive damage to the national economy might be sustained in this area.

Of the million and a half people employed in the floodable area of London, the interruption of work for the whole would probably be only for one or two days. After that some of those with workplaces in the upper storeys might start again; but for those who work at or below ground level the interruption would be much longer. Commerce would be very seriously affected by the disruption of telephone services. It is not possible to estimate the cost.

No mention has been made of insurance in this assessment. Whether any property is insured against floods or not is immaterial when considering damage to the national economy. Some reinsurance might have been effected abroad, which would reduce the immediate damage, but would mean that rates for this service would rise.

Even with the best warning arrangements some loss of life would be almost inevitable. Direct damage would be of the order of £1000 million at 1966 values. Indirect damage due to interruption of business, especially difficulties with telephones and the electricity supply in the nerve centre of the country, would be very great. It was not unreasonable to estimate the total damage at £2000 million (at 1966 values).

4

Aftermath of the 1953 disaster

London was spared disaster in 1953 but the situation could easily have been otherwise. Was the threat taken seriously before that event and what action was taken after this ominous warning?

In the Middle Ages, one suspects that floods were taken as one of the hazards of life, along with plagues, fires and other Acts of God. During the 19th century it was seen that the levels of exceptional surge tides were increasing, and after the two record tides of 1874 and 1875 Parliament acted by passing the Metropolis Management (Thames River Prevention of Floods) Amendment Act 1879. This Act made the Metropolitan Board of Works (MBW) responsible for prescribing flood defence levels throughout London and required riparian owners (a great deal of the river frontage in London was in private hands) to raise their flood defences to these levels at their own cost. Failure to do so permitted the MBW to carry out the works and to recover the cost from the owner of the property. The Chief Engineer of the MBW suggested that the flood defence level should be a foot above the highest recorded tide. The 1881 tide pushed this level up to 17 ft above OD(N). This statutory level was uniform from Woolwich to Teddington. Later, however, the 1928 high-water level showed that, with high fresh-water flow from the upper Thames, levels upriver could be 1 ft or more higher than downriver. In that flood, walls were overtopped in the Hammersmith area, and overturned and breached at Millbank. Widespread flooding occurred and 14 people were drowned, mostly sleeping in basements.

Following this, the Ministry of Health (which at that time incorporated those functions of government concerned with local authorities) assembled a conference. A document was issued, 'Report of a Committee Appointed at a Conference of Public Authorities to consider the question of Floods from the River Thames in the County of London'.

Note that the report was from 'Public Authorities' and not from a government department. The Public Authorities were the London County Council (LCC), the Port of London Authority (PLA), the Thames Conservancy (whose area at this time extended through London), the City of London and 14 Metropolitan Boroughs. The Ministry was carefully avoiding getting its feet wet. The philosophy that 'local matters are local matters' was typical of the time.

The Public Authorities appointed a technical sub-committee on which sat the Admiralty Hydrographer (tides), the Meteorological Office (winds) and the PLA and Thames Conservancy (local circumstances). Studies by the Liverpool Tidal Institute were set in motion which blossomed as told later (p. 67). However, the steady worsening of the tides was not yet appreciated. In the meantime the LCC, who had taken over the statutory responsibility from the MBW, took heed and raised flood defence levels in the Hammersmith area to 18.17 ft above OD(N) and to 17.33 ft at London Bridge (known as the 1930 statutory levels).

Then came the floods of 1953. These were so serious, with many dead and widespread damage, that the Government appointed a Departmental Committee (the Waverley Committee) to examine the danger and to make recommendations. Appointed at the end of April 1953, they made a preliminary report in July and their final report was issued in May 1954. This was fast work for the investigation of what proved to be a most complex problem.

The promptitude with which this committee reported was due largely to the personality of its remarkable Chairman, Lord Waverley, better known as Sir John Anderson. He was born in 1882 and was educated in mathematics, chemistry and the humanities at Edinburgh University and Leipzig University. Entering the Colonial Office in 1905, he rose very quickly in the Civil Service and was Secretary to the Ministry of Shipping by 1917. He was sent out to be Governor of Bengal in 1932 in view of the terrorist problems there. In 1938 he entered Parliament as an Independent Scottish Nationalist and as war drew near in 1939 he was given the key job of Home Secretary with responsibility for organising the new civil defence arrangements, an appointment which made him known widely through the Anderson shelter. Such was his reputation that, when Churchill and Eden were about to leave for the Yalta Conference, Churchill recommended to the King that if they did not return the King should send for Anderson to be the next Prime Minister. After the war Anderson left politics for industry (Imperial Chemical Industries, the Hudson Bay Company and the Canadian Pacific Railway). Because of his knowledge of shipping he was appointed Chairman of the Port of London Authority in 1946, a body which in those days had much greater influence than it does today.

The Waverley Committee reported on what was then known of the natural phenomena which cause surge tides and how these might interact with a normal spring tide to produce very high water levels in the North Sea. Their recommendation covering this aspect was that further research should be done. They also suggested that an improved warning system should be established.

The proposal was made that London might best be protected by a new type of storm surge barrier across the river, which would normally be open to allow free passage to the tides and shipping, but which would be closed to hold back a surge tide. Long Reach, between Purfleet and Tilbury and about 20 miles downriver from London Bridge, was suggested as a suitable site.

There is sometimes confusion between 'barrier' and 'barrage'. A barrier is a structure that can be used to stop the passage of something, in the case of the Thames Barrier the flow of water; alternatively it can be completely opened, in this case to permit unimpeded passage of shipping—which implies that water can pass as well. In contrast, the term barrage has long been in use for a low dam across a river. There is no fixed height at which engineers would cease to use the word barrage. Normally a barrage would have sluices which would regulate the flow of water at all times, locks being provided to enable ships to pass.

As soon as it was known in engineering circles that the Waverley Committee had suggested that some sort of barrier might be built across the Thames, a number of designs were put forward. These ranged from a vast road viaduct from which two 500 ft sluice gates were lowered, to 550 ft gates lying on the river bed, raised by compressed air. Appendix 1 lists a representative selection of these designs. All used normal engineering techniques, and were massive constructions of steel and concrete. None of them, however, would have been anything like as suitable as the design eventually adopted, unless considerably modified to permit maintenance or to take account of the difficulties of closing against a surge tide current. The final design does not, of course, include a 500 ft opening.

To implement the Waverley Committee's recommendation about further research, the Ministry of Agriculture, Fisheries and Food (MAFF) set up an Oceanographic and Meteorological Research Advisory Committee. This pursued research into the nature of surge tides with the aid of the Liverpool Observatory and Tidal Institute and the National Institute of Oceanography (both now part of the Institute of Oceanographic Sciences).

The significant recommendation of the Waverley Committee, as far as this account is concerned, was that investigation should be made into the possibility of a structure which could stop surge tides moving up the

Thames (referred to as a barrier in contrast to a barrage) and into the alternative solution of raising the river banks all the way along the river. To implement this recommendation a Thames Technical Panel was formed.

It may seem that a great fuss was being made about an ordinary engineering requirement, or perhaps that the matter had been taken over by the Circumlocution Office and was being tangled in red tape and buried under mountains of paper; this was not so. The government was face to face with an entirely new problem. If it took the wrong decision the Port of London might be paralysed—something that Hitler had never quite achieved, despite vast efforts—or, after great expenditure, the structure might fail to stop a surge tide from flooding London. A vast project which had been a complete failure was at this time still in everyone's memory. To fight the food shortages which followed the end of the Second World War, a scheme to cultivate ground-nuts over a large area in East Africa was put in hand without anything in the way of research or careful consideration. It was an immediate and very costly failure.

In this case, proceedings were more cautious. The fast-working Waverley Committee was succeeded by the Thames Technical Panel which was to do more detailed thinking. It consisted of the Chief Engineers of the Ministry of Housing and Local Government (MHLG) (which exercised those functions concerning local authorities formerly exercised by the Ministry of Health), the Ministry of Works (MOW) and the Ministry of Agriculture, Fisheries and Food (MAFF), together with Chief Engineers of five local authorities, the London County Council, the City of London and the boroughs of West Ham, Woolwich and Barnes, and the Chief Engineers of four river authorities, the Port of London, the Lee Conservancy and the Essex and Kent River Boards. There were also representatives of the Admiralty, the Ministry of Transport and Trinity House, together with the Director of the Hydraulics Research Station. Eric Johnson, Chief Engineer of MAFF, was very active on the panel, together with Austin Lane of the MHLG, (the Thames Conservancy was not represented because the responsibilities of that body no longer extended below Teddington).

The terms of reference of the Technical Panel were brief: to make a survey of the existing flood defences in the Thames and to estimate the cost of raising them; and to advise whether, having regard to navigational and other requirements, the question of a structure across the river merited further consideration, and, if the appointment of consulting engineers to prepare a scheme was thought desirable, to advise on their terms of reference. Commenting on these terms of reference, the Panel referred to the 1930s scheme for a barrage across the Thames with locks—a fixed barrage instead of a movable or openable barrier. They said, 'The proposal to build a barrage which would permanently impound the river on its upstream side raises issues and affects interests much wider than those we have had to consider in dealing with a movable structure, the latter being quite different in purpose and conception from a barrage'. ('Movable' should quite obviously have been 'openable'.)

In 1954 the Port of London Authority was carrying out a hydraulic investigation of siltation in the Thames Estuary and they had built two small models of it at the Royal Docks. It was on the smaller of the models (horizontal scale 1:3200, vertical scale 1:120) that Alan Price, then working at the PLA and subsequently at the Hydraulics Research Station, first tried out the idea of a barrier. His first model was a roughly cut piece of hardboard shaped to the cross section in Long Reach. Once it was clear that undesirable secondary effects were unlikely, further tests were carried out.

The Report of the Waverley Committee was published in 1954. The Technical Panel started work two months later. The floods had been in February 1953 and, considering the many interests involved and the way in which some of these interests conflicted with others (in particular the navigational interests which were basically opposed to any obstruction in the river), things had been moving quickly.

Nothing has been said about the proceedings and recommendations of the Waverley Committee, except as it affected the Thames Barrier. Nine tenths of the Committee's work was concerned with flood defences on the east coast and with their financial implications. The committee was largely administrative and non-technical in its work. It did, however, make an important recommendation:

'That the maximum standard of protection to be afforded by public authorities against flooding should in general be that sufficient to withstand the flood of January 1953, and this should be provided where flooding would affect a large area of valuable agricultural land, or would lead to serious damage to property of high value such as valuable industrial premises or compact residential areas. Elsewhere the defences should be of a standard which would reasonably have been thought adequate before the flood of January 1953. In certain circumstances higher or lower standards may be appropriate. Anyone requiring a higher standard should pay for it himself.'

The Waverley Committee, in recommending a standard of the 1953 surge tide levels, probably did so in the belief that 1953 was so bad that nothing worse could possibly happen. The Technical Panel, looking at the conditions which caused the surge, appreciated that things could easily have been worse and saw the need for a much higher standard for the densely built-up area of London where so much was at risk.

'The matter of the height of a possible surge was considered and we came to the conclusion that to provide against the worst that might happen a flood-water level of about six feet above the 1953 level should be taken as the possible figure.'

The figure of 6 ft above the 1953 level was arrived at by adding the height of the 1953 surge to that of a spring tide; in 1953 the maximum part of the surge had not occurred at the top of a spring tide.

The navigational interests within the Panel, of which the principal was the Port of London Authority, asked that, to allow ocean-going shipping to pass any structure that was to be built across the Thames, there should be two clear spans, each giving a 500 ft opening either side of a central pier, together with two side spans 250 ft wide, one adjacent to each bank, for barges and small craft. They asked that the vertical clearance should be 220 ft, although this was later reduced to 175 ft, above OD(N). They also specified that the structure should be built in the middle of Long Reach, which would give the maximum possible straight length in which a ship could line itself up in order to pass through the barrier.

At the Long Reach site the river is approximately 2300 ft wide. The river bed is about 43 ft below OD(N) and the crest level of the barrier was to have been at 22 ft above OD(N). When operating against a maximum assumed surge tide, the barrier would be holding up 65 ft of water on its downriver face. There would of course be some depth of water against its upriver face: this would depend on the stage of the tide at which the barrier had closed, and on how much that had changed due to the levelling out of the long pool upriver of the barrier, together with the effect of fresh-water inflow from the upper Thames and various tributaries entering the river below Teddington. But the barrier site at Long Reach had a great advantage in that arrangements to stop flood water passing round the ends of it would be comparatively inexpensive. There is high ground within half a mile of the river on each bank, so that the wing walls could be short. The geological conditions for the foundations of the structure were suitable, with sound chalk at a convenient depth. (The Dartford tunnels are very close to this site.)

There was an alternative to a barrier: the raising of existing flood defences. In London these had just survived the 1953 flood with very small overflows. The target figure for the defence of London put forward by the Technical Panel was 6 ft above the 1953 level. To obtain protection equal to that given by the barrier all along the river, parapets along the great embankments and elsewhere along the wharves and warehouses would have to be raised by 6 ft. The Panel thought that this

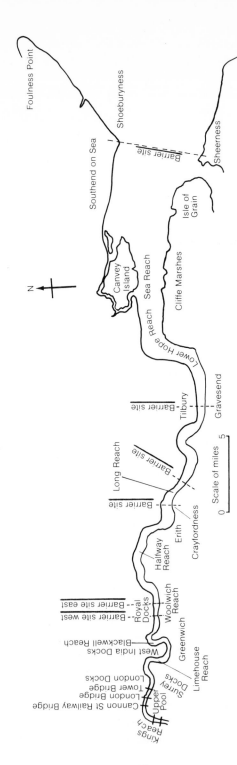

Proposed barrier sites

was obviously impracticable and therefore, merely for purposes of comparison, made two estimates of costs. Raising the defences by 2 ft would have cost £9.3 million; raising the defences by 3 ft would have cost £11.5 million. The many difficulties involved in organising this sort of work, among hundreds of different private frontages, were pointed out, and the Panel could not estimate the cost of claims by frontagers for having their properties made less convenient. Another great disadvantage of the scheme, which does not figure in the report, was that a very large number of openings would have to be left, to enable goods to be taken in from wharves and jetties; the arrangements for closing these openings with temporary stop logs might sometimes fail.

The Panel was unable to give an estimate of the cost of building a barrier, but they thought it would be more or less comparable with the cost of raising the flood walls. A barrier would give protection against floods much higher than those provided against by the 2—3 ft raising of the flood walls, and its construction would not interfere with frontagers. In contrast, the raised flood walls would have unfortunate effects on private and public amenities, blocking the view from riverside properties and walks and seriously interfering with boating and yachting interests along the river.

The Panel strongly favoured the barrier against its alternative and said that a panel of consulting engineers should be appointed to consider the possibilities of the Long Reach site (20 miles below London Bridge) and make recommendations. It was not intended at this stage that there should be a detailed design; rather that alternative possibilities with estimated costs should be put forward for consideration by the Ministry of Housing and Local Government. This Ministry had become the authority concerned with the barrier because of its local authority functions. When the Waverley Committee was formed, the responsibilities for dealing with the 1953 floods had been divided. The Ministry of Agriculture, Fisheries and Food had responsibility for the River Boards while along the coast local authorities, Boroughs, Urban and Rural Districts had responsibility for coast protection (for preventing the sea from encroaching on the land). The River Boards had responsibility for preventing rivers from flooding agricultural land, so they dealt with flood banks down river estuaries and along the adjacent section of the coast. In London, the London County Council (later expanded to the Greater London Council) dealt with river banks inside its area. Outside the LCC area the London Boroughs whose areas touched the river dealt with their own flood defences. The Waverley Committee had contained representatives of these Boroughs as well as the LCC and of course the River Boards adjacent to the Thames. These local authorities and the River Boards were financed by rates and precepts aided by grants from their respective ministries.

The MHLG was the successor to Boards and Ministries watching over some of the activities of local government. This function had become important when local authorities gained powers to borrow money. In this way, members of a council at the time that a loan was incurred could saddle their successors with the repayments for many years ahead, up to 60 years in some cases. Back in the middle of the 19th century some of these councils were small, inexperienced bodies. Few of them had the sort of technical advice which was desirable for large engineering schemes. An inspectorate of qualified civil engineers was therefore formed in 1848 to have a look at such schemes and report to the Government on whether they appeared technically and financially sound. This inspectorate was at first largely composed of retired officers of the Royal Engineers, many of whom had been concerned with engineering schemes of a nature similar to those that they were now to examine when they had been working in India or the Colonies. As time went on a wider range of engineers was recruited, men who had obtained a varied experience of work abroad. Later still, when some local authorities had competent engineering staffs, men from these joined the inspectorate while others came from among the consulting engineers.

The sorts of scheme that local authorities were involved in at the beginning of the 20th century included electricity generating stations, gasworks, roads, bridges and above all vast schemes for water supply, which in turn required the construction of extensive sewerage and sewage treatment works. (By 1953 some of these types of engineering had been moved to the ambits of newly created Ministries.) The MHLG Engineering Inspectorate was technically strong and widely experienced, while MAFF had a much smaller body of engineers concerned entirely with land drainage. It was natural therefore that the MHLG should have assumed primary responsibility for something as entirely novel in the engineering world as the Thames Barrier.

In 1965 the Greater London Council succeeded the London County Council; its territory included virtually the whole area that would be protected by the barrier. It had its own strong engineering department which did not need help from the government. Responsibility for the barrier therefore devolved upon it. (The powers possessed by MAFF for paying government grants were more convenient than those possessed by the MHLG: grants from the MHLG rarely exceeded 40%, but what was needed in this case was something of the order of 75%. After the passing of the Barrier Act, responsibility for the barrier within the Government passed to MAFF.)

Following the recommendations of the Technical Panel, the Minister of Housing and Local Government, with the advice of the President of the Institution of Civil Engineers, appointed two firms of consulting engineers, Rendel Palmer & Tritton, and Sir Bruce White, Wolfe Barry and Partners. Both firms were widely experienced, particularly in dock and harbour work. Rendel Palmer & Tritton had been responsible for much of London's docks. Wolfe Barry had been Resident Engineer on Tower Bridge, and Bruce White had been given a knighthood 'in the field' by Churchill for his work on the Mulberry Harbour, a vast wartime project which required, as did the Thames Barrier, much original thinking. Although the Technical Panel had recommended that three firms of consulting engineers should be appointed, the Government, with cost in mind, appointed only two.

Their first action was to direct some tests by the Hydraulics Research Station on a model of the Thames Estuary made available by the Port of London Authority. This was in fact the same model that had been used by Alan Price in the initial demonstration of the feasibility of a barrier. The tests were directed to finding out what happened when a barrier closed, and particularly to discovering the effects of any reflected wave.

If a stop board is dropped into a flowing channel, the momentum of the flowing water makes it pile up against the board. The accumulation of water then dissipates itself by sending a reflected wave back along the channel. Thus a barrier across the Thames, closing against a fast flowing tide (a tide that could reach 7 ft per second) although protecting the areas upriver, could send a reflected wave back downriver which might overtop the banks there. This reflected wave was a problem, if a soluble one, for the engineers, but to the downriver public it was a real bogey.

Joe Otter, a brilliant mathematician and a partner in Rendel Palmer & Tritton, devised a mathematical model of tides in the Thames Estuary. This was fairly simple in outline, and is described here. Sadly Joe Otter died soon after this model was devised.

The estuary is divided into segments of a convenient length. From soundings and measurements of the shore for a few feet above high-tide level, cross sections of the river can be plotted for the ends of each segment. With these and the length of the segment, the volume of water in the segment can be calculated for any tide level. Conversely the change in water level in the segment can be calculated for any inflow or outflow of a known volume. The model can be made to start operating with, say, the water levels in each segment at low tide. They are not, of course, the same all the way down the estuary because of the effect of fresh-water flow over Teddington Weir, to which must be added the remains of the last tide as it runs out. If the sea level rises above the level of water in the outermost segment, there will be an inflow across the mouth of the estuary. The amount of this inflow in a unit of the model's time scale can be calculated, and so the rise in level in the outermost segment is known.

From that the inflow into the penultimate segment is known, and so on all the way up the estuary. Of course, another interlacing and counter calculation must take account of the fresh-water and residual tidal flow coming down the estuary.

So far so good, but the calculation requires the use of coefficients representing the roughness of the bottom and the degree of indentation in the shore, etc. For the first runs of the model an estimated value is used for these. The first run can start from actual tidal levels measured at the mouth of the estuary. The computer will then calculate the changes in level all the way up the estuary. These are compared with what happens when the real tide flows and the coefficients are adjusted to make them match. This process may have to be repeated several times before the right result is produced. Then the model is tested with different tides until it works well for spring tides. It is then reasonable to expect that if it is fed with the rise in sea level of a really strong surge, a surge stronger than has yet been experienced, the model will give the enhanced surge levels all the way up to the tip of the estuarial trumpet in London with reasonable accuracy. Other matters, such as how the level of the surge in London would be affected by overflows across the flood banks lower down the river, can also be investigated (this was done and the unlooked-for results are recorded later). This technique was developed from the linear flow in a river to the multidimensional flow between one section of sea and another as the tides flow. It has been used to reproduce the tides in the whole of the North Sea, and to reproduce the tides in the Irish Sea for the benefit of the Severn tidal power scheme.

After the 1953 floods, contact had been made with the engineers of the organisation responsible for flood control works in the Netherlands, the Rijkswaterstaat. Whereas London is at the head of a long trumpet-shaped estuary which magnifies its tidal range, Rotterdam is 20 miles inland along a parallel-sided canal which diminishes tides that enter it. The normal tidal range at the entrance of the canal is only 4—5 ft. The Dutch engineers had a problem similar to that caused by the River Thames, but on a smaller scale, in protecting the River Ijssel leading in-land beyond Rotterdam from sea flooding. They only had to provide for navigation by barges and small ships in this channel so their solution was a single drop gate, 265 ft wide, spanning the waterway. A lock alongside permits navigation when the drop gate is closed. The Netherlands' gigantic flood prevention works, which have enabled so much land to be reclaimed, are vastly larger than the Thames Barrier. They fight the waves rather than contend with a trumpet-shaped, tide-multiplying estuary such as the Thames. The Schelde estuary can pose a similar problem, but the effects are felt only when the river reaches Belgium, when the vast port of Antwerp can be affected. The problem there is not as serious as that presented by the Thames. The Belgians are still considering the idea of a barrier.

The problem the consulting engineers had to solve would have been simple if they had been allowed to build a bridge a few feet above the high-tide level, from which a drop gate could be lowered to close the channel. But when the barrier was open, shipping had to be able to pass and so a permanent low-level bridge was not a feasible option. The consultants considered three possible ways of 'removing' the bridge.

The first proposal was for a lifting bridge: there is such a bridge at Middlesbrough, and others around the world. Towers on each bank of the river have a steel span suspended between them. When in use the bridge sits on supports at a convenient low level. When shipping has to pass the bridge is hoisted into the air by winches in the towers. For the Long Reach proposal, the required span of 500 ft offered no difficulty, nor did the required clearance of 175 ft above OD(N). There would have been five towers to accommodate the two 500 ft and the two 200 ft openings. The sluice gates would normally have been hoisted up inside the steel girder work: they would have formed a very heavy but acceptable load. When the barrier was closed and resisting a high tide there would have been enormous sideways pressure on the bridge, but again an acceptable one. The sluice gates would have dropped down on to a concrete sill built across the river. The gates for the proposed Thames lifting bridge barrier would have been 74 ft high by 34 ft wide. The upper half of each gate would have been covered in fixed plating. The lower half would have been rolling gates which would close gradually after the sluice gates were firmly down on to the sill. The sill would resist part of the sideways load.

The second proposal for getting the bridge out of the way was more in keeping with existing bridge engineering practice: to build a swing bridge. There are many examples of this type of bridge, although none with such wide openings as would have been necessary over the Thames. The girders would have had to resist the weight and sideways loads already mentioned and the bridge would have been much heavier than the heaviest in the UK, the swing bridge which carries the Bridgewater Canal across the Manchester Ship Canal. There would have been three swinging spans each with two 250 ft arms, one on each of the piers separating the 250 ft barge channels from the 500 ft ship channels and one on the central pier. The 250 ft arms would link their ends to span each of the 500 ft ship channels.

The third proposal was to build a retractable barrier: two enormous girders, each 930 ft long and 83 ft wide, would have been mounted on wheels, the axles of which would have been set in the concrete abutments. The girders would have been pushed forward from each

34

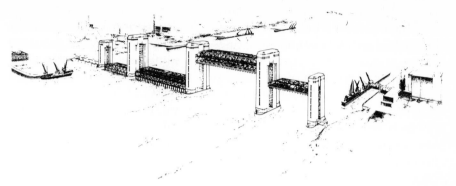

Long Reach: lift barrier (reproduced by permission of Her Majesty's Controller of Stationery)

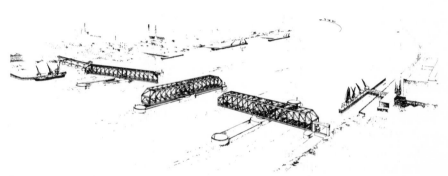

Long Reach: swing barrier (reproduced by permission of Her Majesty's Controller of Stationery)

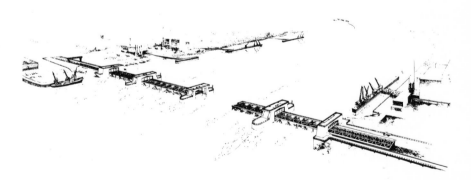

Long Reach: retractable barrier (reproduced by permission of Her Majesty's Controller of Stationery)

bank, over more wheels on the intermediate piers; they would finally come to rest on the central pier. Just before they landed on the central pier, these girders would have formed cantilevers projecting 500 ft, but that would not have involved stresses greater than those dealt with in a girder bridge with a span of 1000 ft, something well within the capabilities of the technology of the time (alternatively, the spans could have been supported by floats as they moved out, the floats passing through channels cut in the intermediate piers). Retractable bridges after this style have been built, but they are small. The longitudinal movement of such enormous girders was not likely to have been as free from difficulties as the straightforward lifting or swinging of smaller girders. These schemes would have involved many more complications than are indicated in this simple description.

In their report the consultants foresaw many difficulties. Cost estimates at 1958 prices were:

lifting type	£15—17 million
swing-bridge type	£13—15 million
retractable type	£15½—17½ million.

If any scheme had been sanctioned the consultants would have required two years for further design work; they thought that construction would take 4½ years. These proposals were set out in a Blue Paper, No. 956 of March 1960. A steering committee was now set up to guide further work by the consultants. This had representatives of the MHLG, MAFF, MoT, LCC, PLA, Trinity House, and the Kent and Essex River Boards (time had passed since the disaster of 1953. Note the slower pace: the committee was set up in August 1961).

5

The 1965 proposals
at Crayfordness

The Port of London Authority now stated that since 1954, when it had agreed to a structure with two 500 ft openings and two 250 ft openings in the middle of Long Reach, it had sanctioned the construction of jetties close to the site. Ships arriving at these jetties turned round in Long Reach and therefore required the Reach to be unobstructed. The barrier could not therefore be built at this site. Seven years and a considerable sum of money had been wasted.

The PLA now suggested a site at Crayfordness, on the bend at the head of Long Reach. In view of the navigational difficulties ships would have while negotiating the bend, they asked for a single unobstructed opening of 1400 ft. This was about twice the length of the ships using the river. The consulting engineers said that they could prepare a design to meet this requirement, but that it would be at the limits of technology. They were asked to prepare outline designs and estimates.

In demanding a 1400 ft opening at Crayfordness, the PLA had stimulated the production of designs which, for their vast scale, novelty and ingenuity, rivalled any hitherto made by civil engineers; the only parallel for size and degree of innovation was perhaps the Mulberry Harbour, with its miles of breakwater towed across the English Channel, its storm-proof floating roadways and its 'spud leg' supported pierheads. (The North Sea oil platforms later presented problems of similar magnitude.) Other civil engineering structures, such as bridges and dams, had been built in gradually increasing sizes; in the case of the Thames Barrier, an immense structure would have to be built on entirely new principles without the help of previous smaller examples. With no possibility of a central pier in the river, the swing-bridge principle was impossible. Bridge spans of 1400 ft have only been achieved by the arch, cantilever or suspension methods, so that a lifting span of this size, which would have had to be a girder bridge, was virtually out of the question. This left the retractable girder as the sole choice.

Consider for a moment the problems involved: stand on the river bank at Crayfordness and look across half a mile of turbulent surge, rushing in at perhaps 5—6 knots. The permanent structures that are to be built must have a gap of a quarter of a mile between them. The girders must be thrust out rapidly to meet across the gap and then sluices dropped to close it. How is a movable cantilever projecting 700 ft to be supported? It would be equivalent to the fixed cantilevers of the Firth of Forth railway bridge. Apart from the stresses due to the overhanging weight, how can the immense lateral pressure of the tide be resisted? The vertical dimensions are equally impressive. The sill level, which is at the level of the self-maintaining bottom of Long Reach, is −45 ft OD(N). The mean high water of spring tides is +12.5 ft OD(N). The design provided for holding up a surge tide at 23 ft OD(N), or a difference of head of over 20 ft between upriver and downriver water levels depending on upriver levels. The load could not be transmitted spanwise to the abutments, but would have to be passed directly from the girder to an underlying sill. A further requirement of the PLA caused difficulties: there could not be any obstruction in the opening during construction bigger than a bucket dredger.

The Consulting Engineers' reports were received on the last day of 1965. Part of the delay was due to the amount of investigation that had proved necessary on the models at the British Hydromechanics Research

Crayfordness: low-level retractable barrier (courtesy of Rendel Palmer & Tritton)

Crayfordness: high-level retractable barrier (courtesy of Sir Bruce White, Wolfe Barry and Partners)

Association to solve vibration problems and so on. Each firm put forward its own design and each found points of difficulty in the design of the other. The two designs are described in Appendix 2. In both designs girders are thrust out from dry docks at each side of the river to meet in the middle. When the girders are in position the sluice gates contained in them are dropped, thus stopping the tidal flow. In both designs the girders have arrangements for transferring the thrust of the impounded water to a concrete sill formed in the river bed. However, that is as far as the similarity goes.

The designs were made on different assumptions. Rendel Palmer & Tritton produced what was called the low-level design. They assumed that it would be possible for the girder to be supported by large pneumatic-tyred wheels, running along the underwater sill. At its front end powerful jets of water would blast away any silt while solid obstructions, for instance, an anchor or a small vessel, would be thrust aside by a great ploughshare. This design required a rather elaborate sill on which a vertical surface to receive the horizontal thrust of the girder had to be formed to within fine limits. This sill was to be built under water by using the girder itself to carry successive precast sections from the shore to their final position in the river. Sluice gates, which would be in their open position as the girder travelled outwards, would be closed when it was in position across the river.

Sir Bruce White, Wolfe Barry and Partners thought that the risk of some massive object, say a sunken vessel resting on the sill, should not be accepted. They therefore proposed a high-level girder which would travel across the river above the water level and then lower the sluice units on to the sill. The sluice units would be frameworks hinged to the

39

girder and when in position would rest against steel abutments built into the sill. Once the unit was in position sluice gates would slide down to cut off the flow in the river. As the girders would have to cantilever outwards to a length of 700 ft their strength would have to equal that of a 1400 ft span girder bridge, something that has not yet been built. As in the case of the low-level design, the girders would be housed in dry docks at each side of the river. The arrangements for launching such girders had, of course, to involve very heavy mechanical engineering. The sill would be built by dredging a trench across the river and using a movable platform supported on spud legs (after the style of some oil drilling platforms) to pour concrete down 'tremie pipes' and allow it to set under water. During the discussions on these schemes Harold Scrutton was specially active on the part of Rendel Palmer & Tritton, as was Alan Beckett for Sir Bruce White, Wolfe Barry and Partners. Estimated costs were (1965):

	High-level scheme	Low-level scheme
Consulting engineers' estimates	£39 000 000	£23 000 000
Other items	£2 250 000	£1 550 000
Total capital expenditure	£41 250 000	£24 550 000

In their respective reports each firm of consulting engineers expressed reservations about the practicability and safety of the alternative scheme, although it seemed that in each case these objections could be overcome.

Faced with what was in 1965 terms enormous expenditure, and with the risks of building to the very limits of the technology of the day, the government paused to take breath; would it all be worthwhile in financial terms? Two lines of enquiry were therefore followed—what would be the cost of flood damage in London and what was the statistical chance of the flood occurring? With these two items of information it would be possible to make some sort of insurance assessment. The potential cost of damage in London was assessed at about £2000 million at 1966 prices (see pages 18—22).

6

The Bondi Report

In the light of the damage estimates other methods of preventing surge tide flooding were investigated again. The possibility of saving Central London by deliberate overspill lower down the estuary was again examined and found to be impracticable. Fixed or movable obstructions in the form of jetties or groynes, leaving a free channel for shipping but offering a sort of frictional obstruction to incoming surge, were considered; neither numerous small jetties nor a few large ones were regardedas practicable. A scheme for a barrage from Clacton to Herne Bay was proposed. This would impound large fresh-water lakes, helping with water supply problems in East Anglia, and would enclose one of the sites proposed for London's third airport, at Foulness. This was regarded as too massive a scheme for the economic climate.

The possibility of a fixed half-tide barrage was investigated. This would have maintained a level of about half tide in the river above the barrier by letting the natural water flow out during the low tide period. 'Flat iron ships' which brought coal from the east coast ports to the upriver power stations could only pass under the Thames bridges at half tide. There were also complications about the supply of cooling water to those power stations. Although a barrage would have led to siltation problems in the river below it, a half-tide barrage would have created smaller problems and, depending on the way in which the outgoing tide might have been discharged, there was some possibility of sluicing any silt deposited because of the barrage down the river. However, a barrage with locks, although no detailed design was made, did not look a good competitor against a completely openable barrier.

In arriving at an estimate of the probability of a surge tide, there was available the work of the Oceanographic and Meteorological Research Committee appointed by MAFF to implement the recommendations of the Waverley Committee in 1953. Much good work had been done. In December 1953, a number of papers were read at the Institution of Civil Engineers including one by Cmdr W.W.I. Farquharson. At the mouth of the estuary, Southend—Sheerness, the average high spring tide level is 10.5 ft OD(N). Cmdr Farquharson, working on somewhat imperfect records from 1820 onwards, found 100 tides which exceeded 11 ft OD(N), the highest being 15.40 ft OD(N). (The excess levels would of course be considerably raised as the surge passed up the trumpet-shaped estuary, and would be much greater than 11 ft OD(N) when they reached London). These records provided the data for two later papers on the probability of high surges, by Dr H.E. Hurst in December 1957 (unpublished) and Cmdr C.T. Suthons, MA,RN, in 1963.

Dr Hurst plotted the height of surge tides against their number and concluded that the probability of a surge tide coinciding with a spring tide sufficiently to produce a level of 23 ft OD(N) in Long Reach (6 ft above the 1953 level) was only 1 in 2000 in a single year. However, as he had long experience of these sorts of calculation, he thought it wiser to assume a probability of 1 in 1000.

Cmdr Suthon's paper was produced for the Oceanographic and Meteorological Research Committee, and dealt with the frequency of occurrence of abnormally high sea levels on the east and south coasts of England. He plotted the 'return periods' for surge tides of given heights, that is the number of years of observation divided by the number of times the given height is reached or exceeded. Using mathematical methods devised by Gumbel and Jenkinson (and including the 1965 tide which was almost a repetition of the one in 1953) he concluded that risks of tide levels in any one year were as follows:

Tides reaching the 1953 level	1 in 100
1953 level plus 1 ft	1 in 350
1953 level plus 2 ft	1 in 1200
1953 level plus 3 ft	1 in 4300
1953 level plus 3.7 ft	1 in 10 000

A factor which may not have received sufficient weight in both of these papers is the gradual sinkage of south-east England compared with the sea level. According to Ordnance Survey records this sinkage is at a rate of about 1 ft per century (see p. 10), but it is believed to be irregular. There is a considerable discrepancy between these two calculations.

An engineer, if asked to throw some light on the problem of if and when a dangerous surge tide might occur, would perhaps tackle the problem on different lines. He might say that the 1953 flood was the worst tide ever experienced: London should, with its raised banks, survive a repetition of that tide. However, what of the tendency for the tides to become higher? He might draw a diagram showing the highest tides against the passing years; this, with data from 1790, would show that the height of the highest tide is increasing at a rate of 2.4 ft per century. The extrapolated line would show the tide overtopping the river walls in Central London in 1953 and rising more than 1 ft above them by the year 2000. Looking at the plotted tides, the engineer might say that seven of these highest tides had occurred over 163 years, about one every 25 years. On that basis, another highest tide could be expected around 1980–1990.

One of the most interesting features of the barrier project arose through argument about the correct way to use the calculation of-probabilities. Economists wished to balance the estimated damage against the degree of probability multiplied by the cost of preventing it. This is a sort of converse of the basis of insurance. Engineers, however, looked at the progression of ever-higher surge tides; to them it seemed that the tide was going to cause a flood in a decade or two, and that if this was so then something should be done about it. The economists' method is certainly applicable to calculations dealing with large numbers, and would be relevant in life assurance or car insurance. It does not seem applicable to isolated or infrequent events such as high surge tides. It would be fruitless to balance the extra cost of making San Francisco's buildings earthquake-proof against the risk of another big earthquake there. It is assumed that an earthquake will happen and the buildings are therefore constructed to withstand one. Catastrophe cannot be quantified. Economists do not consider this argument to be conclusive and so refined probability calculations have been made. However, it is not universally accepted that in this sort of case probability calculations are appropriate guides. The tide levels had risen about 4 ft in 160 years, about 2.4 ft in a century, and the sinkage of land with respect to the sea level was about 1 ft per century (see p.10) which leaves a difference of 1.4 ft unexplained. It has been suggested that this difference might be accounted for by an increase in the range of tides as they pass up the estuary. This has been caused by the changes in the estuary described above (p.16). They have produced a faster current resulting in a greater pile-up of water when the incoming tide reaches the top of the estuary; in other words, a higher tidal range in London.

The first barrier site proposed, in the middle of Long Reach, had seemed satisfactory in every way, until the new jetties were built there. It was now realised that too little consideration had been given before the next site proposed by the PLA had been accepted. The narrower ship channel above Greenwich of 500 ft, or the channel above Limehouse of only 400 ft, began to look attractive. There were problems with these sites. If a structure were to be built higher up the river, there would be the extra cost of raising the flood defences over the stretch of river the barrier would not now protect. This downriver area was, however, almost entirely lined by factories; here access to shipping was by offshore jetties, rather than by wharves close against the river bank. Moreover, most of the flood defences were earth banks and it would not be very expensive to raise these by tipping additional earth or by building low sheet-piled walls along their crests. In this area there would be none of the environmental problems that would have been posed by raising the flood defences upriver to Tower Bridge; the only sensitive area would be the beautiful waterfront at Greenwich.

At a variety of sites on the upper part of the river it would have been possible to build a barrier with a 450 ft or 500 ft opening. This structure could have been of the lifting bridge type; the design would not have needed any new technology and the cost would have been a fraction of the cost of the first design in the middle of Long Reach, which had included two 500 ft spans as well as two of 250 ft. However, when these ideas were put forward they were turned down on planning grounds, as the structures would have been about 240 ft high and 500 ft or more long.

There is often much controversy in considering what engineering structures are not admissible in a non-industrial environment. Battersea Power Station, for instance, is a massive lump of engineering planted in an area of great importance dominated by the Houses of Parliament; the crude power station was given architectural treatment by Sir Edwin Lutyens, who had done the same for the standard Post Office telephone box. Tall brick chimneys used to be the emblem of 'dark satanic mills', but times have changed. Today the disused power station is a listed building. Tower Bridge is an extreme example of a structure 'dressed up' in architectural features. It is certainly an intrusive building as it totally dominates the Tower of London, one of Britain's most important old buildings. No-one complains of that domination today. Indeed Tower Bridge has become even more of a symbol of London than the Tower itself. Yet it would certainly have been a difficult morsel for the planners to swallow, had there been planners when it was built.

The 240 ft high barrier that was turned down by the planners would have been built in an area that was dotted with multi-storey blocks 150—200 ft high in the 1960s. It is difficult to see how a structure urgently needed for flood prevention could be barred on such shallow aesthetic grounds. The area now has a look of desolation, not improved by the disorderly grouping of multi-storey blocks. In contrast, the town planners have allowed St Paul's Cathedral to be submerged by a clutter of office blocks. They have, however, saved the vast area of London's docklands from a massive barrier structure.

By the mid 1960s the method of loading and unloading ships was changing. Since merchant shipping began—some of the earliest was between Minoan Crete and Egypt—cargo has been stowed in the belly of a ship, and later, when ships were decked, in holds. Once this was done by the crews, but more recently the dockers had taken over this work, heaving, pushing and levering the heavy items from where the crane had deposited them into different parts of the hold. It was a tough, unpleasant job, relieved only by the matiness of the gang; and, after the post-war reorganisation of dock labour, it was extremely expensive.

Much of this disappeared with the container revolution. Containers are large, strongly built boxes 20 ft or 40 ft long with a standard cross section of 8 ft by 8½ ft; they have fittings that enable them to be picked up by a crane. These are packed with goods, preferably at the place where the goods are produced, and taken by rail or truck to the container terminal, a part of the port where there is sufficient depth to float ships of 50 000—100 000 t in front of the quay and where there is a large area of flat land behind it for container storage. The vast cranes, specially built to handle containers, can lift from the storage area and deposit in the ships' holds, or vice versa. When the holds are filled it is sometimes possible to carry additional tiers of containers on a ship's deck.

What used to take weeks of manual labour is now done in hours. With turn-round times measured in weeks the few extra hours spent in navigating the Thames did not matter. But with turn-round times measured in hours they matter quite a lot. Moreover, with express trains and fast lorries, the distance between port and final destination is not of great concern: London could now be as well served from downriver quaysides as from quaysides within sight of Tower Bridge. The Port of London therefore opened a container terminal downriver at Tilbury. Within a few years the world's greatest port (and ports were very labour intensive) had shed much of its labour, and had left London. Its going cast a blight over the docklands and this was to have an unfortunate psychological effect on the labour force that later built the barrier.

A number of the upriver docks, starting with St Katharine by Tower Bridge, had gone out of use by ocean shipping, or were about to do so. Shipping was concentrated at Tilbury. However, a few ships still went upriver to private jetties, and there was an increasing traffic of small ships loaded with dredged gravel and sand for use in concrete, as well as the barges carrying 600 000 t per year of London's refuse. In view of this reduced traffic, and after experiments with model ships in a hydraulic model of the river, the PLA was more disposed to accept narrower openings in a barrier situated above the Royal Docks.

The MHLG had now before them the proposals of the consulting engineers, the estimated cost of flood damage, the far-from-simple probability calculations, and the estimated costs of several different

45

schemes. The project had arrived at a critical point in its history. So far it had been propelled by the impact of the 1953 floods. But this initial impetus was running out and it was now on the periphery of MHLG activities. It was obviously less vital than the national housing problem, or indeed less important than many of the problems of local government. It had moved through committees, panels and reports by consulting engineers. Potentially expensive projects are not close to the hearts of government departments; both the expense and the getting involved in something new are disliked. If such a project has no political value, and therefore no sponsorship from the top, it may be in a bad way. The barrier suffered from all of this, but underneath there was still a feeling that something should be done.

In 1966 Sir Solly Zuckerman, later Lord Zuckerman, the Government's Principal Scientific Advisor, was consulted. He had held posts in the upper echelons of the government machine for many years and had gained immense experience in how to make that machine work; he had become a sort of *éminence grise* in the corridors of power. It might well be asked which branch of science had enabled him to go so far through this maze. Sociology is an obvious choice, but sociology has become more of a pulpit than a science. He was in fact a zoologist, and had made his name with a book on the social behaviour of apes. From the *melange* of meteorological and oceanographic evidence laid before him he immediately picked out the significant item: the steady rise over the 170 years for which records were available of the levels attained by surge tides in London. He proposed that a report by a high-ranking scientist, a man of Nobel Prize calibre with a powerful intellect and no preconceptions, should be obtained.

Professor Bondi, FRS, FRAS (later Sir Hermann Bondi), an astronomer, who was then Professor of Mathematics at King's College, and was at various times Director of the European Space Research Organisation, Chief Scientist of the Ministry of Defence, Chief Scientist of the Ministry of Power, in charge of the investigation into the Severn tidal power scheme and Master of Churchill College, Cambridge, was asked for such a report. He examined the various scientific papers dealing with the surges and the plans and estimates already gathered around the project. He was taken to see what the Dutch and Belgians had done or what they had in mind at Rotterdam and Antwerp. (The correspondence with the Dutch had come from the Ministry of Housing and Local Government; when the Dutch engineers asked the Ministry's representative how it came about that a vast river engineering work was in the hands of the Ministry of Housing, Professor Bondi immediately said, 'Don't worry about that, I'm an astronomer.' The Dutch ceased to worry!)

46

An inspection of the Thames was arranged for Professor Bondi. The PLA lent their steam yacht the St Katharine for the purpose. The small party had a good view from the bridge and excellent service from the steward, and they inspected various possible sites. The new and less rigid policy of the PLA, under which they were willing to accept narrower openings in a barrier across the upper reaches of the river, gave increased possibility of an economic solution. Of the alternative sites, the one at Woolwich seemed very much better than the others, especially as it was not far upriver so that the cost of bank raising would not be excessive. The land which it would be necessary to use for construction on both banks of the river at the Woolwich site was vacant, or seemed likely to become so.

In his report Professor Bondi dealt first with the need for a barrier, secondly with what other interests were involved and what general type of barrier would be appropriate, and thirdly with the location, design and character of the barrier.

He had before him such calculations as had been made of the probability of a flood and of the damage it would do. From these an actuarial decision could be made. Also put forward was the view that an actuarial calculation was only suitable when dealing with a large number of events, such as traffic accidents or burglaries, and that catastrophic flooding was more or less a singular phenomenon resembling the incidence of earthquakes. Moreover, the steadily rising surge tide levels over 170 years were a clear indication that something ought to be done. His report said that 'such a problem always raises issues of an almost philosophical kind'. He explored the problem together with its side issues on that basis, concluding, 'I have no doubt whatever in my mind that such a major surge flood in London would be a disaster of the singular and immense kind I have been discussing earlier. It would be indeed a knock-out blow to the nerve centre of the country. The widespread flooding of buildings, with the documentation on which so much of the life of the country depends, would be one major point, but an even greater one would be the closure for a period of many months (perhaps not much short of a year) of the Underground railway system of Central London'. After considering the various probability calculations he said, 'The ominous rise of the highest flood levels over the last 150—170 years must not be left out of account.'

His report went on to consider the possible amenity aspects of a barrage as opposed to a barrier but concluded that a barrage scheme could really only be successful in the context of a major revision of British shipping arrangements and would require expenditure on an unacceptable scale.

The report discussed various sites for a barrier along the whole of the

47

river down to Long Reach in considerable detail. Its conclusions were:

'The extremely severe effects on the life of the country of a tidal surge appreciably higher than that of 1953 (or 1965) makes it appropriate to take preventative measures, even though the probability of a high surge is not great. The most economical defence compatible with the navigational requirements is a retractable barrier in the Dagenham or Woolwich regions. A permanent barrage with locks in the Woolwich region, though markedly more expensive, would materially add to the amenities of London in addition to being a flood defence.'

The very clear lead given by Professor Bondi that the avoidance of a catastrophe was far more important than the calculations of probability and cost—benefit ratios was very valuable. The view that the decision should be taken on the basis of mathematical probability was regarded as a scientific one. The view that, on the evidence of rising tide levels, a catastrophe was far from unlikely was regarded as merely engineers' rule of thumb (although engineers regarded it as common sense). The report made it clear that the non-actuarial conclusion was a suitable one because the case was unusual, and that the thinking behind it should not be adopted when considering an issue where there was massive statistical evidence on which to base a conclusion.

Professor Bondi's report stated the considerations which should govern the choice of site and listed several good possibilities; it did not, however, firmly recommend any particular site. Nevertheless, at the conference on the bridge of the PLA yacht the choice of site was virtually made. Everything was set in motion again.

In the report there was some good advice for engineers involved in similar projects. The PLA's requirements had been accepted by the MHLG; however, it would have been better to argue that the cost of meeting the PLA's expensive demand should have been balanced against the cost to shipping of having to put up with whatever trouble was caused by the inconvenience resulting from adoption of a cheaper solution. 'The navigational requirements were simply accepted and the problem was handed to the consulting engineers giving these requirements as accepted and necessary conditions.' This criticism is very valid. However, to have avoided this criticism, first an estimate would have had to be made of the cost to shipping of the inconvenience caused by the cheaper solution; secondly this continuously running cost would have had to be balanced against the extra capital cost of the more expensive solution, and this in an age of rapidly changing money value; and third the 'inconvenience money' would have had to be distributed among the various possible recipients.

So far as the Thames Barrier is concerned, the Professor provided a solution which is given in the following:

'Of course if sacrifices are demanded from the navigational interests, they must also gain some of the benefits of the savings made. If by accepting a reduced width, say, £4 m could be saved then the question to the mariners should be, 'If of the £4 m saved half was spent on further facilities downstream from the barrier, would this make the entire Port of London more or less attractive than the wider opening without these extra facilities?' Everything has a price and it is only right and proper that, if shipping is prepared to pay part of the price in accepting a reduced opening of the river, some of this saving should come back to shipping in other ways, so that the attraction of the Port of London to shippers is increased rather than diminished'.

In the general way this is an interesting thought. Can one offset a claim for 'injurious affection' by offering a compensatory advantage somewhere else? Could one, for instance, deal with an environmental lobby who protested that a haunt of some rare bird would be destroyed by a project, by offering to construct an area with similar artificial features somewhere else? Such offers have been made. Unfortunately much 'protest' is not so much intended to preserve some such bit of living nature, but rather to prevent anything from being built that is large and technological, those qualities being regarded as unnatural and so objectionable. To the great relief of those engaged in driving forward the Thames Barrier project, no little fish got in the way. Fish of any sort were only just coming back to that part of the river. There is a possibility that the barrier might someday be used to secure environmental advantages by keeping the unsightly mud banks in the river covered with water at low tide. This could, however, generate protests from the lovers of *Arenicola marina*, a small worm that might be injuriously affected by this action (although greater protests could well come from those who wanted to dig up the little worm for bait).

Four men in the public eye were concerned with the Thames Barrier project. Lord Kennet, better known as Wayland Young, a writer on social questions, was the Parliamentary Under Secretary at the Department of the Environment for the Labour Government between 1966 and 1970. On the change of government in 1970 he was succeeded by Eldon Griffiths, a journalist well known for his appearances on television. Both these men had pushed the barrier forward: the project had no political undertones. Richard Adams, who leapt to fame as the author of 'Watership Down', was the Assistant Secretary who watched over the barrier (although his chief love was perhaps English literature). The approach to his desk was difficult—the way through the jungle of large-leaved plants which defended his desk had to be known. Once there, and a few

A.P. Herbert with the authors (courtesy of Hydraulics Research Ltd)

Shakespearean matters disposed of, whatever was necessary for the barrier was quickly settled. A.P. Herbert (A.P. Haddock of 'Punch'), author of numerous books and musical comedies, sender-up of all sorts of puffed-up people and social reformer, was also always available to help with the barrier project. In the First World War he had served with the Royal Navy; in the Second World War he had served with the Thames Emergency Service and the Naval Auxiliary Patrol, which enabled him to mess about in small boats in his favourite area. Later, as a well known river yachtsman and River Conservator, he was looked upon almost as Old Father Thames himself.

So far the project had passed through the hands of ad hoc bodies, the Waverley Committee and the Technical Panel. These committees had no statutory existence, powers or finance. When money was needed for the investigation it was supplied by the MHLG; no requests were refused. Austin Lane as Deputy Chief Engineer of MHLG made considerable contributions to the project in the earlier stages, and Sir Brian Hayes as Permanent Secretary of MAFF, with his grasp of the problems, was invaluable during the complex negotiations in the later contract stages. Adequate technical engineering assistance was provided by the Consulting Engineers and when they in turn wanted an expensive tidal model this was authorised. The MHLG exercised general oversight of the project; that meant that part of the time of an engineer and a small part of the time of an Assistant Secretary were devoted to it. Contact with the Hamburg authorities and inspection of the area affected there to establish the cost of compensation issued after the Elbe flood, and its comparability with the area at risk in London, was made by one of the authors when on holiday. When the PLA quoted the River Eider, in Schleswig Holstein as a case where a barrage had caused the silting up of an estuary, the investigation of that river was made in the same way. In modern terms, the barrier was not an 'in house' project.

In the administrative sense the project fell between stools. It had been the concern of many bodies but the responsibility of none, except, in the most general terms, of the MHLG. When a great emergency occurs the government machine generally responds rapidly and sometimes on a massive scale, but it steps out of its wicket to do so. No legislation required the immediate action the government took to assist the areas flooded in 1953. In cases like this it is sometimes necessary to legislate retrospectively, to cover what has been done. In the case of the Thames flood danger, the preparations to prevent it happening again had gone on for nearly 20 years. But faster action was now to begin.

Cabinet authority had been secured for the necessary expenditure. The local government boundaries across which the project had lain had gone. The Greater London Council had been created to absorb the smaller London County Council and virtually all of the boroughs affected by flooding. The project moved from its ad hoc parents into an organisation equipped with a highly competent executive engineering department, a different matter from the advisory Engineering Inspectorate (at the MHLG) which had hitherto fostered it. The way was open for a more comprehensive investigation and for more rapid progress.

7

Flood precautions

It was obvious that while the extensive investigations and alternative designs were going ahead, the flood might arrive. An elaborate set of precautions was drawn up to prepare for this, most of the work being done by the GLC. The first thing required was a warning system.

MAFF had lost no time, following a recommendation in the report of the Waverley Committee, in setting up an efficient surge tide warning service. Surge tides are caused, as already described, by atmospheric conditions far out over the Atlantic. The information constantly arriving at the Meteorological Office enables these conditions to be detected at an early stage, and the warning service to be activated. Information from a series of tide gauges, starting from the Hebrides and continuing down the east coast to the mouth of the Thames, is passed by direct line or radio to an operations room at Bracknell where, in addition to MAFF officials, scientists from the Admiralty Hydrographers Department come on duty.

Information on the height of the tide is compared with that of the predicted astronomical tide of the day, and the extra height due to the surge is obtained. The service is therefore able to make early and generally accurate forecasts of the time of arrival and the height of the crests of the surge tides as they move down the east coast. Information is passed from the operations room to points where there is a risk of flooding, for example, Hull (now protected by its own sluice-type barrier). The information goes to the police, water authorities and port authorities.

In the case of London before the barrier was operable, the next step was to warn the public of any danger. The wartime air-raid sirens had been maintained in good working order by the Home Office. With suitable publicity, and following tests and demonstration soundings, they became the warning medium. Warnings would also be given over the radio and television networks and by loudspeakers in the streets.

The police planned to move extra men and vehicles into the threatened areas. Observers would be placed to watch for any actual incursion of the water over the parapets. Arrangements were made to bring in small boats from lakes and parks, and for refreshment of the men on duty.

The London Fire Brigade would have a major role in the rescue of people and in sandbagging to block the movement of water. Later they would be involved in pumping water out of basements and sluicing mud away. The London Fire Brigade would be reinforced by fire services from other areas. Plans were also made for bringing into London powerful paraffin heaters to dry out buildings. Stocks of these were held by the armed forces for various reasons and such heaters were also available on hire.

Working parties from the GLC and boroughs would stand by ready to strengthen river parapets suspected of weakness, to stop flood waters invading districts where this was practicable and to repair breaches as rapidly as possible. During the 1928 floods people sleeping in basements had been drowned. Publicity campaigns were started to inform the public in the threatened areas of this danger. As the depth of water would hardly anywhere reach first floor level, except possibly in the Isle of Dogs, the advice given was to take refuge above first floor level. The population contains old or infirm people who might not take notice of a warning or might be incapable of moving. The social services recorded these and made arrangements for their safety.

People whose homes were flooded would become refugees. The social services listed buildings where they could be accommodated outside the floodable areas, such as schools. Arrangements were made for the provision of food and bedding, partly with the aid of voluntary services.

If things were mishandled, large numbers of people might be trapped and drowned in the Underground. London Transport set up arrangements for clearing all trains, passengers and staff from the very extensive area which might be flooded (as noted above, this extends from Hammersmith to Stratford and Kings Cross to Clapham, including the whole of the central and most important part of the network).

A novel, 'The deluge' by Richard Doyle published in 1976, gives a fascinating but somewhat lurid account of what might happen during such a flood. It is ardently to be hoped that nature does not try to better, or even equal this fiction. The flood levels supposed in it would even drown the barrier.

To ensure that the public was aware of the danger and the arrangements to meet it, and to practise these arrangements, the GLC ran a publicity campaign and arranged an exercise at the beginning of each season of risk—in October. These exercises obtained wide publicity in the media. This, together with practice soundings of the flood warning sirens, ensured that few residents of the area would be ignorant of the dangers or of the action required to evade them.

Indeed throughout the progress of the barrier project the media were very helpful. A flood coming in from the North Sea to drown part of London had not been an easy danger to publicise. Perhaps the greatest help given was in the supplement to a Sunday newspaper which showed, pictorially, the then current arrangement made by the Underground for protecting its passengers and network—an employee looking over the river parapet at Embankment Station to watch the rise of the river waters.

The Underground had not been alone in failing to understand the true extent of the danger. Lord Kennet discussed the matter with the Metropolitan Police at their New Scotland Yard headquarters in Victoria Street. The Deputy Commissioner outlined the police plan, laying emphasis on their excellent communications network. He was reminded that there might be several feet of water in Victoria Street and that the public electricity supply would probably be cut off. However, the police Superintendent in charge of communications interposed that they had emergency diesel generators in the building. Asked if these were in a safe location he said they were with all the other communications apparatus on the top floor. When this was challenged by the MHLG engineer who accompanied Lord Kennet as an unlikely location for diesel engines, the Superintendent reaffirmed it. Only when the engineer insisted was the Superintendent told to go and look, when of course he found them in the basement. Some work was then done to prevent flooding of the basement, but later the flood precautions centre was moved to a police station outside the floodable area.

Preparations had been made for dealing with the possibility of a flood occurring before the barrier had been completed. But it was also felt that some form of temporary solution might be possible. The possibility of preparing an inflatable fabric dam was investigated. Such dams had been used, on a much smaller scale, to control flood water in California; in Norway they had been used to increase the depths of rivers, so that logs could be floated downstream; it had been proposed to use a similar system to save Venice from flooding. But extended to the dimensions of the Thames, this technique proved quite impracticable: the design was abandoned.

Another design using the available modern technology for a temporary structure was produced by Professor A.N. Schofield, then at University of Manchester Institute of Technology. Types of fabric had been developed which have very high tensile strength and great resistance to abrasion. These have made possible such things as inshore inflatable lifeboats and the huge sausage-like petrol tanks capable of holding many thousands of gallons; similar fabrics are now also used to reinforce the foundations of a roadway over soft ground.

Professor Schofield's ingenious design was based on the use of these fabrics. A vast fabric sheet was to rest on the bed of the river (it could be removed for maintenance during the summer non-surge season). The upriver edge of the sheet would be linked through running gear to a heavy hawser or cable, both sheet and cable spanning the river. The sheet could be raised by winches on the river banks hauling in the cable. Other cables attached to strong anchors in the bed of the river downriver would be secured to the main cable across the river. By underdraining below the sheet and pumping, the lower edge of the sheet would be gripped between the water pressure and the river bed. As the surge came in the depth of water and holding pressure would increase. The underdrainage would be formed by perforated plastic pipes inserted in layers of clean gravel dropped into a trench dredged across the river bed. Any silt settling on the sheet could be tipped off it by raising the sheet on the outgoing tide. This was an unusual solution and had its attractions, but in the event it was decided to raise the flood defences throughout London by 1.5 ft as an emergency measure. This work was carried out in 1971–72 (Chapter 13).

As well as preparing for a possible flood before the barrier had been completed, it was important to allay fears that the actual building of the barrier aroused.

One matter that loomed very large in the investigations regarding the barrier, a sort of ghostly opposition, was the reflected wave (the wave itself could of course be real; it was widespread unfounded fears of it which were ghostly). If the movement of water in a fast-flowing channel is suddenly stopped, there will be a pile-up of water in front of the obstruction. This 'heap' of water has, in due course, to find its own level and this it must do by some of it moving backwards. This pushes the pile-up effect further and further back down the channel, the effect diminishing with distance. To the onlooker it seems that a wave has started at the obstruction and is moving back down the channel. The height of the pile-up in front of the obstruction (the closed barrier) will depend on the speed at which the current was flowing. Should there be a quick-action closure of the barrier near the top of an incoming surge, when the tidal level was already high and perhaps about to overflow the banks downriver, then the rise in water level due to the reflected wave would cause an overflow. In other words, if wrongly operated, the barrier could make things worse for downriver areas. Most of these areas are low lying and only protected from normal high tides by their flood banks.

Canvey Island had much to fear: surrounded by water, with flood banks all round, no high ground on which the population might seek refuge and only one road out to the mainland, it was already very much at risk. Moreover, it had suffered many deaths in 1953. Its justified fears spread to neighbouring areas, even though these were not subject to anything like the same degree of risk.

The case has been set out here as the downriver populations saw it. A closure could produce disastrous effects. However, if the closure were made at low tide with ample clearance between water levels and the tops of the flood banks, then as the tide rose the dynamic effects of sudden closure of the barrier would have decayed whilst the tide levels were low and safe.

Even this small effect could be diminished. A normal high spring tide does not cause flooding in London. Therefore the entire volume of a normal high spring tide could be let past the barrier without trouble. Even against a surge tide the barrier could close slowly and no high 'dynamic' pile-up of water downriver of it would occur. If the barrier were going to close slowly it would have to start in ample time, in other words, well before high tide; so the warning system would be essential to give ample notice of the surge.

The downriver population could, of course, argue that the warning system might fail. It was necessary to explain that the warning system started to work the day before the surge, when there were unfavourable meteorological conditions in the Atlantic, and that the incoming tide was monitored hour by hour as it travelled round the north of Scotland, down the east coast and finally up the Thames Estuary. It could hardly make that long journey unobserved.

There was another fear in the mind of the public. If the Thames were blocked against an incoming tide by closure of the barrier, it might be thought that the outgoing flow of fresh water would also be blocked and that this might result in overflows inside London. Also, the sort of weather which would produce a surge tide might also produce heavy rainfall, thus making things worse. There are some grounds for this fear as there is a tendency for heavy rainfall at these times. However, the area of the impounded pool behind the barrier is so vast that even flows over Teddington Weir at the recorded maximum would have only a minor effect.

8

The GLC investigation

Following the passage of the London Government Act through Parliament, the Greater London Council was set up and took office on 1 April 1965. They had inherited from the London County Council their powers under the Thames Flood Acts. Keen to measure up to their new responsibilities, they immediately started pressing the Government to take action over the Thames flood problem, as they had the statutory responsibility under the 1879 Thames Flood Act. Once it was known that Professor Bondi had submitted his report the Council, on 21 November 1967, resolved to press the Ministry of Housing and Local Government to expedite the publication of their report on the feasibility of a permanent barrage and/or retractable barrier in the Thames Estuary. This was in view of the considerable public anxiety about the risks of extensive flooding in London. The Ministry informed the GLC that the detailed engineering studies they had commissioned had shown that a movable flood prevention barrier in Long Reach, providing a clear 1400 ft opening for shipping, would raise great technical problems and be extremely expensive; a further study (the Bondi Report) had suggested three other sites above Long Reach, where construction of a movable barrier might be less difficult and less expensive.

On 29 January 1968 the Ministry followed this initial reply by inviting the GLC to undertake an urgent investigation into the construction of a movable barrier at each of three suggested sites: just below the Ford works at Dagenham, just below Dagenham Dock, and in Woolwich Reach; and a fixed barrage above the entrance to the Millwall and India Docks, with provision for the passage of barges, and possibly small ships, only. Following urgent discussions, agreement was reached on the general terms and conditions under which the GLC was willing to carry out the investigation. The relative advantages of the two types of structure at the locations suggested, together with the strengthening of riverside defences below the structure, were to be the basis of detailed study. At the same time the GLC intended to investigate other suitable sites and means of flood prevention. Its investigation would take into account current development proposals for the riverside area of Greater London, the long-term plans of the Port of London's shipping interests, the possibility of combining a new river crossing with a barrier or barrage, and the implications of any of the proposed measures on flood defences elsewhere. The GLC emphasised that the investigation was intended to resolve the complex issues in the shortest possible time, and that a firm decision would be taken and put into effect on conclusion of the investigation.

Within the GLC the investigation was made the responsibility of the Director of Public Health Engineering (then Stanley Dainty) under the political direction of the Chairman of the Public Health Services Committee (at the time Peter Black), and the necessary organisation was carried out in co-operation with the MHLG. A great deal of work had to be done and to save time many studies were run in parallel, whereas it would have been more logical to run them in sequence.

To direct the organisation a Policy Committee was formed. This was chaired by Lord Kennet, then Joint Parliamentary Secretary to the MHLG, and had representatives from government departments, the Hydraulics Research Station, the Port of London Authority, the Chamber of Shipping, the Kent and Essex River Authorities, and the GLC.

Detail control of the investigation was carried out by the Steering Committee, which was chaired by the GLC Director of Public Health Engineering and representation was similar to that on the Policy Committee. The Public Health Services Committee of the GLC had executive responsibility for decisions and finance: at the end of the day they paid the bills. The Government refunded half of the cost under the grant aid arrangement; any proposal to incur cost therefore required the agreement of the MHLG representative on the committee. Estimates of the cost of the various studies were submitted to the GLC Public Health Services Committee for approval and authority to spend. These administrative arrangements worked well during all stages of the work: feasibility study, design, letting of contracts and construction. This was due in no small measure to the leadership and support of the successive chairmen of the PHS Committee, Peter Black, Arthur Edwards, Maurice Gaffney, Bernard Brook-Partridge, Stanley Bolton and Simon Turney, with backing from their vice chairmen, Andrew Jardine, John Branagan, Bryan Cassidy and Neil Davies.

It was essential to draw on the best scientific and technical knowledge

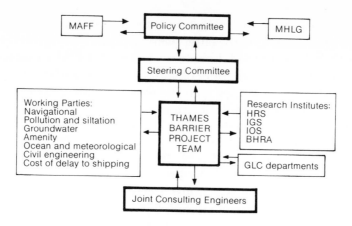

Organization of the investigation

available; working parties were set up for each area of study. Day-to-day direction and co-ordination of these working parties was carried out by a small team of technical officers, headed by Ray Horner as Project Manager. The two most important areas, which required the best possible data, were the probability and magnitude of high surge tides and the width of opening in the structure necessary to allow free passage for vessels (the size and type of vessels, and therefore the size of opening required, would depend to a certain extent on where in the river the structure was built).

To deal with the probability of high surge tides, an Oceanographical and Meteorological Working Party was set up; there were representatives from the Hydrographic Department of the Admiralty, the Institute of Coastal Oceanography and Tides, the Meteorological Office, the Hydraulics Research Station, MHLG, and the Ministry of Agriculture, Fisheries and Food. Of this group perhaps the key figure was the Admiralty representative, Commander Suthons, who had made a detailed study of the incidence and probability of high waters along the east coast, following the recommendations of the Local Authorities' committee which sat after the 1928 floods. Dr Rossiter of ICOT had also carried out valuable research on the adverse change of high waters relative to land levels: this work had a considerable effect on the government departments concerned who were forced to realise that, at least with this problem, time was not on their side.

The meteorological aspects of the working party's brief were also important. Dr Lamb of the University of East Anglia had proposed a theory that over the past decade depressions had been taking a more southerly route across the Atlantic. This could have a significant effect on the probability of surge tides, and meant that yet another factor had to be added to the brew. Were the odds lengthening or shortening? It looked very much as if the latter were the case.

The working party had the onerous but vital task of assessing the current probabilities of surge tides of various heights, and the magnitude of the increase of high waters with the passage of time. Much work was done, records researched, instrument errors assessed, probabilities discussed. Two areas were particularly problematical. Smaller surge components, that is the increase of water level over the normal predicted tide, had been experienced with the higher surge tides. Was this a physical effect related to the hydraulics of the water movement in the southern North Sea, or was it just a matter of probability: fewer high predicted tides and therefore less probability of a big surge occurring on a high predicted tide? The other important question was the possibility of the peak of the wind-induced surge coinciding with the peak of the astronomical tide. Examination of the records showed that in most cases the peak of the surge arrived between one and three hours before the normal time of high water. Was this just chance or was there some mechanism which caused the surge to avoid high water, or did the combination of surge and normal tide move up the estuary faster than the normal tide? (The high water that arrived early was actually a combination of these two components.) There was never complete agreement on these matters but it was finally accepted that an estimate of probabilities based on observations in the Thames Estuary, provided that it could be corrected for reduced levels due to overspill of flood defences, would have these effects 'built-in'. It fell to GLC Research Engineer Brian Hall to distil all these data, and to produce the master graph that forms figure 7 of the First Report of Studies published in October 1969. His work has

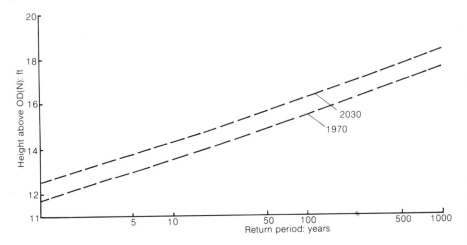

Probabilities of high water at Southend

stood the test of time: in 1978 Dr Pugh of the Institute of Oceanographic Sciences (formerly ICOT) gave, on the basis of a synthesis of the probabilities of surges combined with the probabilities of predicted tides, the estimated level of a high water at Southend with a probability of 1 in 100 in a year; the level was checked against Hall's figure 7 and found to agree to 0.1 m.

A major factor in the cost of any barrier scheme is the width of opening to be provided for the passage of shipping. Advice on this was the responsibility of the Navigation Working Party, on which were representatives of the Board of Trade, the Chamber of Shipping, MHLG, and the Department of Mechanical and Electrical Engineering and the Valuation Department of the GLC: the representatives of the PLA were concerned with the overall navigation problems of the river, but the responsibility of getting shipping through the barrier would lie with the pilots of Trinity House who were therefore also represented. Captain Rees of the PLA and Commander Greenfield of Trinity House were particularly constructive in their approach to the problems considered by this Working Party.

Initial discussions on the width of openings to be provided at the various barrier sites were based on the 427 m opening recommended for the site at Crayfordness, 18 miles downriver from London Bridge at the upper end of Long Reach. For the next site, in Halfway Reach near the Ford works, 305 m was suggested. The figure for Woolwich Reach was 274 m, for Blackwall Reach 183 m and for Lower Pool 61 m, tug assistance to be provided. Lock sizes for barrage schemes at a number of sites were agreed. These were:

Location	Width	Length	Depth to sill (max. water level)
Cannon Street	15 m	107 m	12 m
Blackwall, Woolwich Halfway Reach and	24 m	183 m	15 m
Long Reach	61 m	244 m	18.3 m

This information was passed on to the Consulting Engineers who worked up outline schemes and approximate costs. It was soon apparent that the widths of openings that had been agreed initially were too generous to allow economic structures to be designed. The Navigation Working Party had to have a rethink.

Decline of river traffic to the upriver docks was cited; the future closure of the Surrey Docks and the India and Millwall Docks was a possibility; the navigators saw the point and were persuaded to lower their sights a little. It was suggested that the barrier at Woolwich Reach might have two openings of 137 m instead of a single opening of 274 m.

After consideration of this proposition the Working Party suggested a single central 137 m opening with a 61 m opening either side. They did not like the central pier in the middle of the navigable channel which they regarded as a hazard to shipping. The main opening would be reserved for large vessels, inward bound on the flood tide and outward bound on the ebb. This was agreed.

It was not until much later, after the closure of the Surrey Docks had been announced in the autumn of 1970, that agreement was reached on what transpired to be the final scheme, that of four 61 m openings for a structure at Silvertown in Woolwich Reach.

Besides the size of the openings, the Navigation Working Party was concerned with the level at which the sills for all openings should be set, warning time for shipping prior to the barrier closing, arrangements for mooring vessels delayed by the barrier's closure, and navigational aids and notice boards. One of their recommendations was that the PLA's radar coverage of the estuary should be extended ten miles upriver to Blackwall Point as part of the barrier project.

The possibility of some form of arrester gear, to check a ship which might attempt to pass the barrier when the gates were closing, was also considered (this was well before the accident and damage to the lock gates on the Manchester Ship Canal which led to the installation of arrester gear there). Steel cables were proposed across the river at an angle of 45 degrees to the direction of the main channel. These would normally lie on the bed of the river, but could be raised by powerful winches, with the object of diverting any vessel attempting to pass the barrier into the mud banks on the north side of the river. The navigational representatives were not enthusiastic about this idea!

The Pollution and Siltation Working Party considered whether these problems were likely to arise with a barrier. Representatives were nominated from the PLA, CEGB, HRS, Thames Conservancy, Water Pollution Research Laboratory, MHLG and the GLC. It was thought that operation of a barrier at infrequent intervals would not cause any difficulties from pollution or siltation, although there might be a minor problem with power station cooling water during the closure period. The opinion was expressed that there could be considerable problems of this nature with a barrage.

It was evident from an early stage that opposition to a barrage scheme would be too powerful to give such a scheme much chance of general approval. There was, however, a strong and influential group who favoured the condition of an impounded upper river; but it was also clear that as soon as there was a serious suggestion to impound there would have been a very vocal group against it because of the effect on the ecology of the estuary between the barrier and Teddington Weir.

Operation of a barrier as a tide control structure, in a manner similar to the present mode of operation of the Richmond sluices, would give many of the advantages of a barrage, without the same problems of pollution and siltation. Such a mode of operation would have a great advantage for a flood control structure since the structure would already be closed when warning of a surge tide might be received. Reliability of closure, the Achilles' heel of any barrier, would therefore be much improved.

On the problem of pollution, it was thought that reduced oxygen levels in an impounded river would be the most serious effect. Cremer and Warner, the PLA chemical engineering consultants, carried out a mathematical model study on the change of oxygen levels and river water temperatures upriver with a barrage at London Bridge. These effects were not as bad as certain interests had expected and provided evidence that a tide control structure in Woolwich Reach might be a practicable proposition. The difficulty of any mathematical model was, however, evident: results largely depended on the coefficients of the various formulae fed into the model. Arguments developed on whether, for example, the re-aeration coefficient was too high or too low. Since this was largely a matter of opinion, these discussions tended to detract from the value of the results provided by the model.

The most serious pollution problem with a barrage, and this could apply to a tide control barrier, would be the possible effect of raising ground-water levels in the stratum of Thames Ballast which underlies much of the flood plain, with possibly the resultant settlement of basements and foundations. A Ground Water Working Party was set up. The main input of expertise was provided by representatives from the Institute of Geological Sciences; there were also representatives from the Water Resources Board, the Thames Conservancy, the Building Research Centre, and MHLG. Deliberations proved interesting and revealing. Colonel Gilbert described his observations on the underground movement of water in and out of a river bed consisting of Thames Gravel, and on the ability of a river to waterproof its own bed with silt. It was soon apparent that little was known about the movement of water in the flood plain area of Central London. A number of boreholes were put down with automatic recording level indicators and data were obtained. The interpretation of these data stimulated a good deal of very erudite discussion. It was apparent from the borehole levels that there was a movement of ground water in the Bermondsey area southwards away from the River Thames. At first it seemed that this explained the known higher rate of infiltration in the low-level sewers in South London, but further investigation showed that this was not the case. The water was presumably finding its way down to the chalk, deep down below London.

The approval of the finance for this ground-water study was given in a Policy Committee meeting. Lord Kennet as Chairman was probing the problems of a barrage compared with a barrier. The possible siltation and pollution effects were mentioned. Ray Horner suggested that ground water could be the most serious difficulty, but a research programme was really necessary to investigate this, as so much depended on the subsoil conditions in the flood plain. Lord Kennet's request for an estimate of cost for such a study put Horner on the spot, but he managed an estimate based on a two-second intense mental calculation (no time for pocket calculators, even if they had been available then). The method of calculation was based on putting down boreholes, ten sections across the flood plain, each consisting of ten boreholes. Based on the cost of a bored pile, at that time £100, he decided on a total cost per borehole of £400. Ten by ten by £400 gave £40 000 as the cost of the study. Immediate approval was given and the study went ahead. Subsequently, as a back-up operation, in case questions were asked, Brian Hall, the Research Engineer in the Barrier Team, worked up a detailed estimate for construction, operation, maintenance and reinstatement of a borehole which strangely enough came to £400!

An Amenity Working Party was set up. This was a very important facet of the investigation, as it was vital for public relations that proper consideration was seen to be given to this side of any proposal. The GLC as the regional planning authority was strongly represented here: there were Working Party members from the GLC Departments of Planning, Architecture and Civic Design, Parks, and Highways and Transportation, together with statisticians from the Treasurer's Department.

Initially the civil engineering aspects of the investigation were put in the hands of a joint team of consulting engineers, set up with the two firms involved in the earlier investigation: Rendel Palmer & Tritton; and Sir Bruce White, Wolfe Barry and Partners. As previously described, the two firms had submitted earlier proposals for a barrier at Crayfordness, and therefore had a good deal of background knowledge of the problems. Unfortunately, however, they had submitted two separate and different schemes for the site. This was not the best way to get government to take a decision on a project as important and costly as the Thames Barrier; the setting up of the joint team was thought to be the best way of avoiding a repetition of that particular difficulty.

As the study progressed it became evident that the involvement of a wider spectrum of engineers was desirable, to get as comprehensive a range of views as possible. A Civil Engineering Working Party was set up with members from the joint consulting engineers, the PLA, the British Hydromechanics Research Association, the GLC and the MHLG.

The joint Consulting Engineers were looking at barrier and barrage proposals at a wide range of sites, but it was also necessary to consider the problems involved in raising the banks of the estuary as this could and did influence the choice of barrier or barrage site. A small team of engineers from the Rivers Branch of the GLC took on the responsibility of this task, led by George Thompson, who was the Assistant Divisional Engineer on Thames Flood Protection and who had long experience of the problems of Thames flood banks.

For the purpose of the earlier work following the 1953 surge tide and the Waverley Report on the problem, a physical model of the Thames Estuary had been constructed in a shed in the Royal Docks. This had provided very useful information on tidal movement, on the effect of overspilling the banks in the lower estuary, and on the effect of closure of the river by a barrier structure which was expected to increase levels on the downriver side. It was evident that a new model would be necessary for the GLC investigation, and an early decision was taken to request the Hydraulics Research Station, who had considerable experience with such models, to design and construct a new Thames Estuary model. It was considered necessary to model the whole of the Estuary from Teddington Weir, the normal tidal limit, to Southend. The size of the model would then be fixed by the scale selected. A large-scale model would make the taking of water-level measurements easier and more accurate. On the other hand, a large-scale model would be very expensive to construct and would take up a lot of space. Hydraulic model engineers have a technique which helps to get over this problem; they often use a much larger vertical scale than the horizontal scale. This distortion is actually beneficial in satisfying the conditions of reproducing natural phenomena such as siltation. The decision was taken to use a 10:1 ratio of vertical to horizontal scales. A vertical scale of 1:60 was the smallest for reliable measurements of 0.25 ft, which were required to give a reasonable assessment of the effects of barrier closure downriver (reflected wave effect). This gave a horizontal scale of 1:600. Teddington is 45 miles west of Southend, so the model would be about 400 ft long. It was very desirable to have the model under cover, both from the point of the staff working on it and for reliability of water-level gauges, etc. A number of large store sheds were available at the old army depot at Didcot, which was reasonably near HRS at Wallingford. The CEGB had taken over the area of the depot which included the store shed selected. Arrangements were made to rent the shed for some years. However, there was a complication: the shed was only 380 ft long. The HRS engineers had a simple and ingenious solution. Reversal of the Chiswick bend would make virtually no difference to the performance of the model. This would result in Teddington Weir being set down in Wandsworth, and would shorten the model sufficiently to enable it to be fitted in the shed!

Didcot model of the Thames Estuary (courtesy of Hydraulics Research Ltd)

Construction of the model started in August 1968 and was completed by November 1968. The model was constructed with a cement mortar bed carefully shaped to the cross sections of the river. A tide generator was provided at the seaward end. Water was pumped into the model and spilled over a tilting weir. This enabled normal astronomical tides and any desired surge profile to be generated. This was done either by using a cam shaped to give the correct tide profile, or by a curve reader. The cam was used where many repetitions of a tide were required, and the curve reader to reproduce a particular profile infrequently.

The GLC Public Information Branch (PIB) required the superstructure of Tower Bridge to look like Tower Bridge. This had no effect on the hydraulic performance of the model, but they considered it vital in order to convince the public that the model would give worthwhile results.

Installation and testing of the control equipment and tuning the model to reproduce a normal spring tide took until January 1969. When a spring tide was run on the 'as constructed' model, before it was tuned the effect was comparable with the Severn bore as there was too little friction. The PIB thought this was marvellous for publicity purposes, and took a lot of convincing that surge tides did not look like that in the actual river!

The Liverpool Tidal Institute (now part of the Institute of Oceanographic Sciences) had followed up Joe Otter's original work and had developed a mathematical model of a tidal estuary. Dr Rossiter of the Institute convinced the Project Manager that use of this model could assist the investigation. It was appreciated that the two models were bound to give different results, but some very significant information did emerge when both sets of research engineers were arguing about the correctness of their particular results. Once the working parties had been set up and the model investigations initiated, a period of intense activity ensued. The plan for the investigation was first to assemble the data and to sift and analyse it so that the relative importance of the major factors was understood. All feasible ways of meeting the flood threat could then be considered and those which showed little promise of becoming practicable solutions could be rejected.

The next stage was the detailed assessment of the most promising schemes, leading to a firm recommendation in favour of the best solution. The term 'best' is used in its most comprehensive sense, to refer to the scheme which achieved the best compromise in terms of cost, speed of construction, reliability, running and maintenance costs, and acceptability. Frequency of meeting of working parties depended on the phase of the investigation. Initially, the Oceanographical and Meteorological Working Party was of paramount importance. Once, however, a reasonable basis for the probability of surge tides had been established and the reliability of the warning system which would be required to initiate barrier closure had been assessed, the Navigation Working Party became priority. This working party met on average every two months for at least two years. The other working parties met as necessary to meet the requirements of the investigation. There was a continuous flow of recommendations, decisions, and information back and forth—Policy Committee—Steering Committee—Barrier Study team—working parties—consulting engineers with reports to the GLC Public Health Services Committee and progress letters to London boroughs, riparian county councils, Kent and Essex River Authorities and district councils downriver in areas subject to flooding from the tidal Thames.

By the autumn of 1968 basic decisions for the progress of the investigation were emerging. General opinion in the Policy Committee was coming to the view that a standard of flood defence 6 ft above the 1930 statutory level at London Bridge (which was then some 40 years out of date) was a reasonable compromise between an inadequate short-term solution and a very high standard which would be effective to the end of the 21st century, but which might well appear extravagant to those who had to foot the bill! This gave a level for the defences at London Bridge of 23.33 ft above OD(N). Subsequent analysis showed this simple estimate was a little high compared with the 1000-year return period tide allowing for the adverse change up to AD 2030. This tide would be expected to reach 18.4 ft above OD(N) at Southend Pier. If, however, one foot of freeboard is allowed for wind and wave action, then the differential from London Bridge to Southend becomes 3.93 ft, which can be exceeded with high upland flow or with strong easterly winds in the estuary. The high water which occurred on 31 December 1978 reached 13.1 ft at Southend and 17.1 ft at London Bridge, a difference of 4 ft. This was with upland flow of 183 m^3/s, a moderately high flow, and easterly winds. This situation occurs when the depression causing the surge takes a more southerly course over northern France, rather than the more northerly route across the north of West Germany as in 1953.

Another important decision that had to be taken was on the surge profile which should be fed into the model studies. In 1953 strong northerly winds had blown over a large area for many hours. The surge had lasted over three high waters. A similar pattern had developed at Hamburg in 1962, in that case the second tide being the highest, in contrast to 1953 where the first tide reached the highest level. In 1965, however, a surge developed of fairly short duration which, by the time it arrived in the Thames Estuary, was practically in step with the rising tide. This gave a tidal movement of far greater amplitude than the 1953 type. This could be very significant in the effect of barrier closure. It was decided to use both types of profile for the model experiments.

By the end of 1968, the enemy had been clearly recognised, and his strength and mode of attack identified. Now the problem was to decide on the best form of defence. Was it a matter of flood banks, barrage or barrier, or was there some other form of defence which would be a practical and reliable solution? It was vital to look at all possibilities, since a decision by Council or Parliament could easily be delayed if it could be suggested that some option had been overlooked. The GLC barrier team had brainstorming sessions for an hour or so once a week to try to dream up some really way-out proposal which might be a good answer. The GLC investigation had been fairly well publicised and the general public took a hand with suggestions. One gentleman had a very simple solution—

just dig a ship canal, at sea level of course, from the Thames to the Bristol Channel (very handy for bringing super tankers to London to cut the price of petrol). Since high water in the Thames is at the same time as low water in the Bristol Channel, dealing with a surge tide in the Thames would be a simple matter of opening sluices and letting excess water out of the back door! Peter Shallow, who was the GLC Deputy Project Manager, went to a good deal of trouble concocting sensible replies to all the various suggestions, as a public relations exercise.

An unorthodox method of dealing with the problem was the possibility of increasing the resistance to flow up the estuary. The smoothing of the estuary as a result of flood protection measures was considered to be one of the contributory causes of the adverse change in high-water levels, so why not increase the resistance and so reverse the change? This solution was well demonstrated by the HRS physical model during the 'tuning' stage. Initially the tidal range was far too high because the carefully moulded cement-rendered bed was too smooth to give the right degree of friction. Additional resistance was provided by placing small stones and sections of perforated zinc on the bed until a correct reproduction of the normal spring and neap tide ranges was obtained. This concept, so simple in theory, proved very difficult to implement with a practical scheme. The obvious idea was to construct a series of groynes out into the estuary from both north and south banks to increase the drag on the inflowing tide. However, to be effective such structures would have to extend practically right across the river, obstructing the shipping channel, since the bulk of the flow upriver took place in the deep water of the navigable channel. The idea was then suggested of some sort of 'pop up' structure, and a few sketch plans of suitable devices were prepared. The complexity and the difficulty of maintenance eventually led to the idea being dropped. One suspects the navigation interests would not have been at all enthusiastic about the proposal.

Some serious work was done on another possible method of reducing the flood risk. Work on the first HRS physical model constructed shortly after the 1953 floods showed that the bursting of the banks of the outer estuary and the flooding of Canvey Island and the Kent and Essex marshes had reduced the high-water level in Central London by nearly 0.5 ft. The idea had already been put forward of having an area well downriver provided with sluices which could be opened when a dangerously high surge tide was entering the estuary. Water would flow on to the marshes and levels upriver would be reduced. It would be uneconomic to reclaim an area for this purpose, but if a suitable area of marshland could be made available, this proposal might provide an effective answer. The Cliffe Marshes on the Kent coast provided a large low-lying area, and a model study was run on the Institute of Oceanographic Sciences' mathematical model to investigate the effect of using 6500 acres of this area. The results were very interesting. Using a fixed weir six miles long about 12 ft above mean sea level, useful reductions of level were obtained with the 1953 surge tide. With higher surge tides no benefit was obtained and in certain sections upriver an adverse effect was noted. The overspill operation as run on the model actually increased levels. This was due to the overspill area being filled to capacity. Additional flow was drawn into the estuary due to the lowering of water levels produced by the flow into the overspill area. This increased the velocity and kinetic energy of the in-flowing tide. When the overspill area was full, this additional flow was diverted upriver and because of the greater energy due to the higher flow velocity, levels upriver at the top of the tide could be higher than if the overspill had not been provided. The results for the 1953 tide plus 2 ft, as run on the model, showed maximum levels being reached in the Westminster area as occurred with the actual 1953 tide. This reduction in level did not occur with the 1953 tide when run on the model, as the over-spill weir was set too high (12.1 ft OD(N)) to be fully effective for the particular surge tide. A shorter and lower weir would have been a better solution. This result, however, suggests that the lower levels reached by the 1953 surge tide upriver of Westminster were due to the breaching and overtopping of the flood defences in the lower estuary, although the westerly winds blowing in that area at the time may also have contributed. The general pattern of all tides is to show steadily increasing levels as they pass upriver right up to Teddington Weir. This still applies even when upland flow is low, although the rise is increased when the upland flow is high, as is to be expected.

The initial experimental results suggested refinements of the method. In general diverting flow to overspill fairly early on the flood tide would be more effective than shortly before the peak, provided that the area did not fill up before the flood peak had passed. Lower and shorter weirs appeared promising, but had the disadvantage of flooding the overspill area on lower tides when it was not necessary to bring it into use. This suggested a collapsible weir which would keep out normal high spring tides but could be dropped when a dangerous surge tide was forecast.

It was then decided that the whole thing was too complicated, and not a practicable proposition, particularly in view of the great difficulty in selling the idea politically, since very strong local protests could be expected from the people who lived or worked in an overspill area! The effort put into this study was not wasted, because a lot had been learnt about the hydraulics of tidal flow in the estuary which was useful background information for the other studies which were going on.

Another widely advocated method of reducing the flood risk to London was artificial narrowing of the outer estuary by land reclamation schemes.

On a fairly elementary assessment, it appeared unlikely that any such proposal was really practicable, but it was essential to investigate it, otherwise it could be said that the investigation had ignored a sound and beneficial solution. A model programme was the obvious method of evaluating the possibilities of the method. The HRS physical model at Didcot was not suitable, however, as the tide generator was too close to the eastern end of the model to give reliable results. A suitable program for the IOS mathematical model was set up to investigate the possibilities of this method of reducing the tidal amplitude. The results from the model studies came out much as expected: it was necessary to reduce the cross-sectional area of the estuary by at least 80% to reduce a high surge tide to an acceptable level. Velocities through the opening would be very high, rising to 4 m/s. The structure would have consisted of two long piers running out from the north and south banks of the river leaving an opening in the centre about half a mile wide. The openings in the pier structure would have a number of gates which could be closed when necessary to force flow through the centre opening. This suggestion was discussed with the navigation authorities, who were far from enthusiastic about restriction of the estuary in the Canvey Island—Southend area to a half-mile-wide opening. Extensive bed protection would be required for the central opening to prevent scour of the river bed which would increase the area of the opening and decrease the effectiveness of the control barrier. In concept, the structure would have been comparable with the Eastern Scheldt barrier, although this structure extends across the whole estuary, having 66 openings of 40 m width fitted with sluices which can be closed to seal off the estuary when required.

While these rather unorthodox schemes were being given consideration, work on various barrier and barrage proposals was going ahead with maximum urgency. Six preferred sites were selected for conventional barrages or barriers. Harold Scrutton, the senior partner of Rendel Palmer & Tritton, suggested a 'shopping list' of schemes to allow a preliminary appraisal of possible solutions. A total of 31 different structures were considered, with some of the schemes having two or three variations. Sites ranged from Cannon Street to Long Reach, and designs from barrages with lock systems to simple barriers. Types of structure included low-level and high-level retractable barriers, and barriers with sector and drop gates. The most ambitious proposal must have been the scheme for Woolwich Reach of a barrier with a 750 ft span drop gate, with hindsight quite an attractive proposal with only two main piers and two smaller ones in the river. Preliminary estimates were prepared for each scheme and the whole of the work done with commendable speed.

At the same time the team in the GLC's Department of Public Health Engineering was undertaking the preparation of schemes and estimates

Drum gate at Crayfordness (courtesy of the Greater London Council)

for raising of the banks from Crayfordness to Cannon Street.

By the summer of 1969, it was possible to bring all this information together and to narrow down the range of possibilities. A First Report of Studies was prepared and presented to the GLC committee responsible for monitoring the investigation, the Public Services Committee. The report recommended that further studies should be concentrated on the development of designs for barriers at the Woolwich and Crayfordness sites. A drop gate was proposed for the Woolwich structure, but the feasibility of the Crayfordness structure would depend on the development of a satisfactory drum gate, as this was considered the only type of gate suitable for this particular structure in view of the various constraints associated with the site. A 1400 ft opening was required at this site.

The PLA required obstruction to navigation to be kept to a minimum, comparable with the obstruction caused by a dredger operating in the reach. The drum gate could meet these requirements, but had a number of disadvantages. The gate is sector shaped, and pivoted at the centre of the radius of the cylindrical surface. It is positioned in the bed of the river, lying in a recess formed in a concrete sill with the line of the pivot horizontal and at bed level. The gap between the sector-shaped recess in which the gate lies and the gate itself is closed by a seal. The gate, which is filled with air and buoyant, is held down by the water pressure above, the gate recess being drained to a sump provided with pumps to deal with any leakage. When the recess is flooded, the gate rises due to its buoyancy and the barrier is closed, preventing water from passing upriver. The 1400 ft opening was to be closed by 13 gates, each 109 ft wide, with a 1 ft space between gates. A good deal of thought was given to this structure as the Crayfordness site was attractive in view of the saving of 20 miles of bank raising compared with the Woolwich site. There were two major problems with this type of gate. Each gate had 580 ft of seal which had to be maintained in a watertight condition if the gate were to operate reliably. It was expected that this would be a major maintenance problem. Construction would also be extremely difficult, as the bottom of the excavation for the gate recess would have to be nearly 150 ft below a high spring tide. Sealing the bottom to enable the water to be pumped out of the cofferdam would have been difficult. Sinking of caissons might have been possible but positioning would have to be done very accurately. In view of these difficulties, the conclusion was reached that the structure could not be recommended.

To overcome these objections, the PLA engineers came up with an alternative proposal for the Crayfordness site. This consisted of the construction of a number of gate units which would have been prefabricated in a building dock and then floated out into position in the river and lowered into place on prepared foundations. Each unit would consist of a concrete base and would be fitted with a steel gate which could be raised

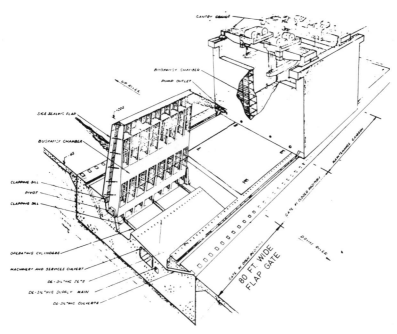

Alternative proposal for the Crayfordness site (courtesy of the PLA)

Drop gate in Woolwich Reach (courtesy of the Greater London Council)

by a hydraulic mechanism. The gates were of similar size to those of the drum gate proposal, and were similar to a lock gate. The steel gates would lie horizontally in the river bed with the pivot on the upriver edge. The hydraulic mechanism consisted of a cylinder connected to the base and provided with a piston and rod connected to the gate in a similar manner to the control mechanism of a lock gate. The cylinder was double acting so that pumping oil into the end furthest from the gate connection would cause the gate to rise. Since the pivot was on the upriver side, the flow of the tide would then help to lift the gate, but there was a difficulty here. The closure tests for a barrier at Crayfordness by the HRS had shown that a big difference in water level either side of the gates built up quite quickly. Provided that all gates were closed in ten minutes there would not be much of a problem. However, if for any reason a gate was a little sluggish and took 20 minutes to close, then very large forces would be exerted, as water levels either side of the gate could show a difference of 10 ft or so. This would produce a force on the gate of more than 1000 tons, which would swing the gate with such speed that the hydraulic cylinder would be unable to check it at the end of the travel of the piston. Serious damage could result and one or more gates might fail. In the space available it was difficult to install cylinders sufficiently powerful to guard against this. There was also the serious maintenance problem of all the cylinders, connecting rods and pipework in the bed of the river. Thought was given to the idea of sealing the gates in their recesses, so that the space under the gate could be drained and access obtained through a tunnel running through all the gate units, but this did not appear to be very practicable. The scheme to install a drop-gate barrier at Woolwich appeared much more attractive, so the decision was taken to concentrate on this proposal, and the idea of a barrier at Crayfordness abandoned.

The structure proposed for Woolwich Reach had a main gate of 450 ft span, flanked to north and south by smaller drop gates of 200 ft span. Four smaller falling radial gates of 100—115 ft span were provided, two to the north and two to the south, to allow free flow of the tide through the structure. There was of course the problem of the thrust of the water against the large main gate during closure. This could have been reduced by providing sluices through the gate which would only be closed after the big gate was safely down on its sill. These would, however, add to the weight of the gate, and would complicate the closure operation. Maintenance costs would also be increased. On balance it was decided not to provide sluices, but to accept the thrust during closure which would be taken by a system of steel rollers mounted on the ends of the gate. An open box girder construction was adopted for the main gate, the downriver face being fully plated with 'Vierendeel' girders* on the upriver side. The girder was counter-balanced with weights housed in the piers and provided with cast iron and water ballast. Twin drive motors were provided and in an emergency the gate could be closed by dumping the water ballast and lowering under the control of large disc brakes. Closing time was estimated at half an hour.

At about the time this structure was being developed, the closure of the Surrey Docks was announced by the PLA. This was taken to indicate that closure of the West India Docks, the next system downriver from the Surrey Docks, could not be very long delayed. Since the 450 ft span was being provided mainly to cater for vessels moving to these docks, there was a case for a review of the size of opening required. There were obvious advantages in dividing the central opening into two smaller openings of 200 ft. All four main gates could then be made the same with obvious advantages in construction and operation. If due to mischance it were not possible to close one gate, the flow of the tide through the structure would be sufficiently throttled to prevent a serious flood upriver. Even on a very high surge only minor flooding would occur.

The idea was immediately accepted by both the Government and the GLC. The problem was to persuade the PLA, pilots and Chamber of Shipping that this arrangement would be satisfactory. The main opening of Tower Bridge was 200 ft and the fact that vessels up to 20 000 t had passed through this opening without too many mishaps for 80 years was

---

* A truss-type girder without diagonal bracing. Stiffness is provided by fixed joints between the vertical and horizontal members.

Rising sector gate barrier: artist's impression (courtesy of the Greater London Council)

a powerful argument in favour of the 200 ft opening.

An event occurred during the Policy Committee meeting of 29 September 1969 which could well have spurred on both the Government and the GLC to reach a decision. Eric Johnson, the Chief Engineer of MAFF, had to leave the meeting half-way through, as a flood 'Danger' warning had been issued for the east coast. Forecast levels for the Humber and the Lincolnshire coast were higher than the levels reached by the disastrous 1953 tide. In everyone's mind there was a real fear of a repetition of the 1953 disaster. The actual level reached at Immingham was higher than 1953 by 0.2 m. Fortunately, wind velocities in the southern North Sea were not high enough to cause any problems in the Thames, but considerable flooding occurred in Hull. In the end everyone agreed on the size of opening and the way was clear for the final scheme to be developed, and for the GLC to obtain powers from Parliament to go ahead and build the structure. The end of the beginning was at last reached.

9

Interim protection,
final barrier design

The GLC's First Report of Studies was transmitted to the Minister of Housing and Local Government in January 1970. In March of the same year, the Minister expressed concern that it must inevitably be some years before a barrier could be completed and the permanent wall-raising carried out to a standard to provide a high degree of protection against flooding. He asked the GLC to consider whether it would be practicable and desirable to undertake interim measures to afford at least some degree of protection to London and the downriver areas until the permanent works were complete. Following a preliminary appraisal of the possibilities, the GLC was asked in May 1970 to undertake at once a detailed study of the problem. The study was carried out and a report was made to the Public Services Committee of the GLC in December 1970. Three main methods had been considered: controlled overspill, temporary barriers and raising of existing defences. The report recommended the raising of flood defences in the GLC area by 1½ ft. This applied to 136½ miles of flood defences involving 2000 riparian owners.

To enable construction to start as soon as possible, design work had to be kept to a minimum. After discussing types of contract, it was decided to call for conventional competitive tenders based on outline designs and schedules of rates with provisional quantities. The idea of a negotiated contract for the whole job was turned down on the grounds that a better overall performance and greater flexibility would be obtained with a number of contractors. The work on the main river banks was divided into eight contracts, varying in length from nine miles to just over one mile. In the Thamesmead area little work was necessary as a considerable amount of bank raising had been carried out in this area after the 1953 floods. The London and Surrey Dock systems were protected by earth dams in the entrance locks as these docks were no longer in commercial use. A special form of caisson was designed by the PLA for the entrances of the West India and Royal Docks. This had a steel frame with reinforced rubber fabric diaphragms, supplied by the Avon Rubber Company. These were manufactured by the British Steel Corporation and Green and Silley Weir. The Lee Conservancy Catchment Board (LCCB) decided to protect the considerable length of tidal walls in Bow Creek by constructing a drop-gate tidal barrier. A small drop-gate barrier was also necessary for Limehouse Cut, otherwise flood water could flow up it from Regents Canal Dock and flood low-lying land in Tower Hamlets. Interest in the main river bank contracts was keen and these contracts were let to a number of medium-sized contract firms. Mears Bros were awarded three contracts on the south bank covering the length from Wandsworth to Woolwich. To avoid problems of access for another contractor, work in the Thamesmead area was carried out by Cubitts under the existing value cost contract which the GLC had negotiated with them for the Thamesmead Development. The longest contract on the north bank was let to Caffin Ltd, and was in two sections, in the Hammersmith and City—Tower Hamlets area. Pritchard and Peach had the contract for the Isle of Dogs section, and Peter Lind the north bank from Bow Creek to Barking Creek. The contract for the important Westminster area was carried out by Kier, which included the Victoria and Albert Embankments. This contract was supervised by the GLC Department of Planning and Transportation, all the other contracts being the responsibility of the Department of Public Health Engineering, who also had the overall co-ordinating role. The estimated cost of the work for which the GLC was responsible was £4 million (including the work on the PLA docks) and the cost of the LCCB barrier for Bow Creek was expected to be approximately £750 000.

At the outset the task appeared daunting. At the time the 'in' thing for civil engineering contracts was to devise a critical path network. This can be a valuable tool, but demands time and effort. Brian Hall, the Research Engineer on the barrier team, was made Project Manager for the interim bank work, and when asked whether he intended to prepare a critical path network for the project, he replied that it was a case of producing the network or doing the job. The question of a critical path network was not raised again! The object was to carry the work out to completion by the flood season 1972—73. The specified contract durations varied between nine months and eighteen months; the problem was to finalise designs, get access and get the work done in accordance with these durations! A good deal of design had to be done 'on site' but this still had to be subject to the normal 'statutory check' as there was little point in raising the walls unless they were strong enough to withstand the water pressure.

There was one very helpful aspect to the problem, however. Over the years the Thames Flood Section of the GLC, who were responsible for checking that flood defences in the GLC area were properly constructed and maintained, had adopted a forward-looking attitude to all applications for redevelopment of river frontages. They considered that the day must come when the statutory levels set for the tops of banks and walls would be revised upwards, and therefore had advised all developers to provide walls two feet higher than the statutory levels. This applied to just under half of the total frontages. In certain cases it was simply a matter of bolting a timber baulk on top of an existing concrete or masonry wall, but in others a careful analysis of the existing structure was necessary, and major strengthening was required before the level could be raised. Arranging access to properties was a major task. Each frontager had to be approached and an effort made to fix an access date which suited the contract plan, but which at the same time was convenient for the trade or business carried on at the particular site.

It was essential to use the staff with a knowledge of the problems of these flood defences to maximum advantage. Teams were built up with additional staff taken on for the purpose, some seconded from firms of consulting engineers with expertise in this field, to service the various contracts. No two frontages were alike, so 1000 individual designs were produced. Some sites posed difficult design problems, either as a result of the use of the site, or the type of construction of the existing bank or wharf. Improved flood defences for the upriver oil depots were particularly difficult because of the complicated pipe work between the shore installations and the jetties. A different kind of problem arose with the defences of the Royal Naval College at Greenwich. The walls here were built with stone very similar to that used in the original construction. In the case of the parapet wall of the terrace of the Houses of Parliament, stone from the same quarry as the stone for the original building was used. For the frontage of the Hurlingham Club, great care was taken in pumping the concrete so that the beautiful lawns were not damaged. Arthur Mascall, the Resident Engineer for that particular contract, said that after the work was done, the Secretary of the Club came to discuss precautions to be taken in carrying out the work and could not believe that the work was already finished!

The walls of the Victoria and Albert Embankments were raised by placing concrete blocks on top of the existing granite copings. The proposal to raise these walls in a similar manner to the terrace of the Houses of Parliament, by lifting the parapet and inserting a course of granite blocks before replacing the parapet, was turned down on the grounds that it would be too difficult to lower the walls after completion of the barrier! The walls were strengthened at the same time by inserting reinforcing rods in drilled holes at about 3 ft centres. These were grouted into the base of the wall using a special synthetic resin grout, and were then post tensioned before being grouted up over their whole length. The whole project went amazingly well, due in no small part to the energy and enthusiasm of the team of engineers working on it. By the end of February 1972, 66% of the properties where work was necessary had defences raised to the new standard. All the bank work was complete by the start of the 1972—73 flood season, and the final item (the Bow Creek Barrier) was operable by early December 1972. The work was carried out within the original estimated cost, the threat of a serious flood had been reduced five fold, and London's flood defences were able to contain a repetition of 1953 in spite of the loss of the overspill which occurred then in the outer estuary. (Model studies of the 1953 flood had shown that if the water which flowed out over the Essex and Kent marshes and Canvey Island had remained in the river to flow upriver, the level at London Bridge would have been higher by six inches.)

Work on the interim flood defences, vital though it was, did not delay work on the main barrier. The GLC decided to appoint Rendel Palmer & Tritton (RPT) to be the consulting engineers responsible for the detail design, drafting of contract documents, letting of the contracts and supervision of the work. Initially Alex Young was the RPT Project Manager, but the post was later taken over by George Carr, after Young left RPT to go back to his old firm in Scotland. A decision was required on the location of the barrier in Woolwich Reach, and on the type of structure to be built.

The most suitable site, in the middle of the reach, was opposite the large Tate & Lyle sugar refinery on the north bank, but the cost of compensation if this factory had been taken over was so large that this site was ruled out. There were two other feasible sites, one about in the middle of the eastern half of the reach and the other in the middle of the western half. The studies for the 450 ft drop gate had concentrated on the eastern site. The site in the western half had certain advantages, however, to be set against the obvious disadvantage of the additional length of bank raising that would be necessary if that site were adopted. The approaches were much better than those of the eastern site, which was too near the bend round Bull's Point from Gallion's Reach and very near the position of the Woolwich Ferry, which was an undesirable feature as shipping would have to negotiate two hazards in the channel close together. Foundation conditions were thought to be slightly better in the case of the eastern site, but this would not be proved until a detailed survey had been done. In the event, the situation resolved itself. Strong objections to the eastern site were raised by the Council of the London Borough of Greenwich, since choice of that site would interfere with a housing development scheme which the Borough had on the drawing board for the old Woolwich Dockyard site on the south bank. Acquisition of land on the north bank would entail taking over an industrial site with some loss of jobs. In the case of the western site, land became available by chance on both banks. On the south side, the AEI (now part of GEC) site at the end of Eastmoor St came on the market as a result of the closedown of the turbine test plant there, and on the north bank the Regent Tar Works site was up for sale. Acquisition of both these sites and some additional land would be a fairly easy matter. The western site was selected and work went ahead to finalise design of a barrier on this site.

The barrier proposed for the eastern site had a central opening of 450 ft and a drop gate was planned for this. The GLC and London Borough of Greenwich planners were not in favour of this design on the grounds of its appearance. There were also doubts about the possible hydraulic vibration of a drop gate as it descended through the rapidly moving tidal water. For the four 200 ft openings of the western site the Consulting Engineers favoured the drum gate in these respects but were far from happy about the deep excavation necessary for its construction. One of their engineers, Charles Draper, came up with the idea of a gate which used the principle but did not require the deep excavation. This was the rising sector gate. This gate is similar in principle to the falling radial gate often used in river control structures, but so designed that in rotating it rises up from the river bed to close the opening between the piers. This is accomplished by securing each end of the gate, which is segmental in cross section, to large wheel-like structures pivoted at their centres. Rotation of these wheels causes the gate to move in a circular arc from its open position in the bed of the river to its closed position between the piers. Further rotation of the wheels brings the gate clear of the water in a position suitable for any inspection or maintenance work which may be necessary.

Not only did this design avoid the deep excavation which would have been required for the drum gate, but closing was a positive action by powerful hydraulic machinery. Thus the final design for the barrier evolved—four main navigation openings 200 ft wide with rising sector gates with a further two 100 ft wide navigation openings also with rising sector gates, one to the north of the main openings and one to the south, for the use of smaller craft. To allow the free flow of the tide through the structure, four more openings of 100 ft are provided fitted with a simpler form of gate, the falling radial gate. Three of these non-navigation openings are adjacent to the north bank and one to the south bank. Control of all ten gates is from the control tower on the south bank.

Once a decision had been taken on the site, a detailed and comprehensive subsoil investigation was put in hand. A preliminary site investigation had been carried out in the area in 1970 as part of the initial investiga-

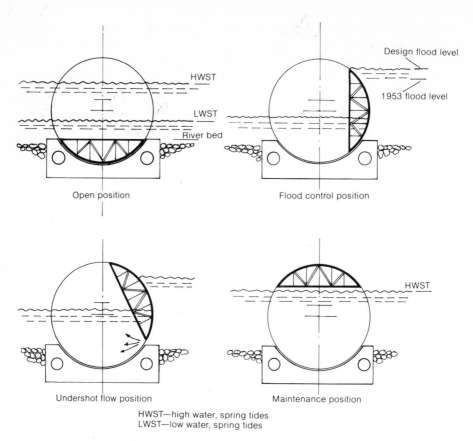

Open position

Flood control position

HWST
LWST
River bed

Design flood level

1953 flood level

Undershot flow position

Maintenance position

HWST

HWST—high water, spring tides
LWST—low water, spring tides

Barrier gate in four positions

tions. Seven boreholes had been put down, samples taken and tests carried out. This work was done by Foundation Engineering Ltd. The further more detailed investigation was again carried out by Foundation Engineering Ltd between December 1971 and May 1972. Seventy three boreholes were sunk, 54 of which were through water. Sixty eight of the boreholes were for foundation conditions in the areas where the piers and abutments were sited, and the remaining five were required for dredging of the proposed diversion channel to enable ships to pass the site during construction. In addition, 17 boreholes were sunk on land on the north and south banks for installation of piezometers and water-level recording equipment for ground-water investigations carried out by the Institute of Geological Sciences. A comprehensive range of tests was carried out both in the boreholes themselves and on samples taken from the boreholes. Tests were carried out to determine the permeability of the Chalk, Thanet Sand and the gravels.

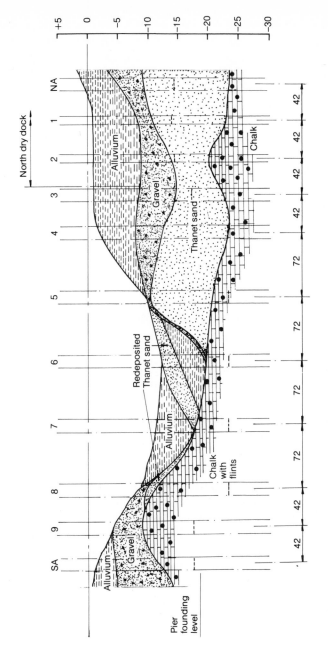

Woolwich Reach: western site, geological section (courtesy of the Institute of Geological Sciences)

A disused sandpit near Maryon Park, Charlton, provided the opportunity for further tests on the Thanet Sand. In-situ density tests were made and samples taken. It had been hoped to expose the Thanet Sand—Chalk interface but this was not practicable. Previously a 4.5 m shaft and boreholes had been sunk in the Upper Chalk at the CEGB site at Littlebrook Power Station for test purposes. Wimpey Laboratories Ltd carried out a water-borne acoustic survey to provide details of sub-river bed features. Two systems with sound energy at different frequencies were used, described as 'pinger' (transducer source) and 'boomer' (mechanical percussive source). The 'pinger' proved more successful, but reliable interpretation of the results was only possible over the southern part of the deep channel.

The detailed site investigation, carried out at a cost of £100 000, showed that the site was underlain by strata of adequate bearing capacity for the foundations of the piers and abutments of the barrier. The Thanet Sand in the northern part of the site was considered suitable for foundations for the northern piers and abutment, and the Chalk for the southern piers and abutment. Precautions to protect the Thanet Sand against scour were advised. Long-term settlement of piers founded on Chalk and Thanet Sand was considered to be negligible in comparison with the elastic deformation under the weight of the piers; it was accepted that some settlement would occur due to the reconsolidation of material at or below founding level which had been disturbed during excavation. Most of this was expected to occur during construction and should not affect the sills and gates which would be installed at a late stage of construction.

The micropalaeontological and geophysical studies established the existence of small-scale faulting, which was not considered to have affected significantly the engineering properties of the materials. It was also concluded that there was little risk of damaging movements from these faults or from the larger faults in the region. The site investigation also showed that there was at the site a general absence of material softened by frost, deep frost shattering and major solution features which are often found in the Chalk in south-east England. Narrow pipes (voids filled with debris) could exist, however, and it was accepted that excavation for the piers could reveal these features.

A number of model studies had to be carried out to check the structural design and the hydraulic characteristics of the gate. The gate itself was a form of box girder and the stress distribution was fairly complex as in the closed position the weight of the gate and the thrust of the water acted at right angles to each other. The curved shape of the downriver face had been adopted to ensure that the thrust from the water passed through the centre pivot of the gate end. This was necessary to avoid any direct load from the water pressure having to be resisted by the operating mechanism. The dead weight of the gate leaf was counterbalanced by cast iron weights fitted into the gate end wheel opposite the part of the circumference to which the leaf was bolted. To reduce the load on the operating mechanism it was decided to allow the gate to flood as it was lowered into the water, and for the water to drain out of special ports in the lower edge as the gate was raised. The gate design was based on a complex finite element analysis by computer of the stresses set up by the dead and live loading. Due to the importance of the project and the intricacy of the design, it was considered advisable to carry out tests on model gates to check the accuracy of the mathematical calculations. In consultation with Dr Dowling of Imperial College, it was decided to construct two models, one to a scale of 1:25 made of Araldite, and the other to a scale of 1:6 made of steel. The 1:25 model was made and assembled in the College laboratories, but because of pressure of work in the College workshops, the 1:6 scale model was constructed by Research Models and Equipment Ltd.

The purpose of the smaller model was to provide a check on the linear elastic finite modelling analysis used for the design of the gate. Two scales were used in this model, for overall dimensions the scale was 1:25, while for thickness the scale was 1:10. The use of two scales was permissible in the structure as it could be regarded as thin-walled. In con-

Barrier gate: steel model (courtesy of Imperial College, London)

structing the model, all components in the actual structure were reproduced. A total of 700 strain gauges were attached to the model for measurement of strains when under test. The model tests showed that adjustments were needed to the original finite element idealisation to give good agreement with the observed behaviour. It was shown that the curved skin of the gate contributed up to 23 % of the total shear stiffness. The larger steel model was constructed to obtain information on the load factors against collapse of the gates. Determination of the ultimate load-carrying capacity of the structure to an accuracy greater than that of the theoretical calculations was essential. In addition a model test tends to be more convincing than a theoretical calculation, certainly to the non-technical! The scale of the model was selected to produce the largest model which could be tested in the Imperial College laboratory, but at the same time the smallest in which the required amount of detail of the structure could be reproduced. The model was first tested with a reverse head loading to simulate the gate being closed with the water level upriver at high spring tide level, while the level downriver was allowed to fall to low-tide level. The model withstood a loading of 1.8 times the live (water) load and 1.2 times the dead load satisfactorily. In the main load test, failure occurred under a loading of 2.17 times the dead and live loads. Early yielding occurred in the end web panels adjacent to the openings in the webs provided to permit water to drain out of the gate as it is raised out of the water. This in turn led to buckling of the curved outer skin at the quarter points of the span, where the plate thickness reduced from 40 mm to 30 mm. As a result of the test, the web openings in the end bays of the structure were omitted to eliminate the area of weakness.

In commenting on these results, Geoff Miller-Richards, the RPT engineer responsible for gate design, remarked that if the simple formula for bending moment in the centre of the gate—load multiplied by span divided by ten—had been used as a means of estimating the stress, the difference in comparison with the computer program's result would have been less than 10%. The other aspect of gate design which required investigation was that of hydrodynamic stability. Unstable flow conditions during closure could lead to forces on the gate which could cause it to oscillate. Needless to say, it was essential that the operating machinery should have sufficient 'muscle' to cope with any such forces. The British Hydromechanics Research Association were consulted on this problem, and recommended the construction of a 1:20 scale model to evaluate any such forces. The first model was constructed in wood and was used to indicate the conditions for which more detailed tests were required. As a result of this work, it was decided to construct a 1:40 scale model of a section of the gate together with a 1:20 scale hydroelastic model of a complete 61 m rising sector gate. The supports of the 1:40 scale model were designed so that the model would vibrate in the same manner as a mid-span section of the gate, at natural frequencies related to the primary modes of vibration of the prototype. The hydroelastic model was designed to reproduce the scaled dynamic behaviour of the prototype for structural vibrations. Rotation of the gate was controlled by a spring system designed to represent the stiffness of the operating machinery. These tests explored thoroughly the behaviour of the gate under a wide variety of conditions, and showed that the forces set up would not be of a magnitude to cause problems under all normal operating conditions.

For detailed investigation of current directions and velocities and for siltation studies in respect of areas of the river outside the navigable channel, the Hydraulics Research Station recommended in June 1971 the construction of a second physical model of the estuary. The horizontal scale for this model was 1:300 and the vertical scale 1:60. The model was constructed in the shed at Didcot alongside the earlier model and covered the length of the river from Tilbury to the tidal limit at Teddington. The model was built with a reduced ratio of horizontal to vertical scales of 5:1 as this would give less distortion of flow round the bends of the river and give better overall reproduction of the velocity pattern. Construction of the model was started early in 1972 and the model was proved and ready for tests by November 1972. Tests were carried out to determine the effect on velocities in Woolwich Reach as a result of the construction of the barrier, both during construction and on completion. Pier alignment, cofferdam design, and dredging requirements were investigated. The HRS also carried out bed protection studies on two further physical models to scales of 1:25 and 1:50. Tests were carried out to determine the effects of normal closure of the gates with undershot flow and the effects of failure of one gate to close. J.S. Burgess was in charge of these studies.

There was a further problem with the design of the gates. This was the method of supporting the shafts about which the gates turned. Initially the intention had been to support each shaft individually. This would mean that any change in the alignment of the piers necessary to suit the flow pattern on both the flood and ebb tides, could be accommodated without changing the alignment of the whole structure. Various designs were proposed, but none was considered satisfactory. The hydraulic model tests were in progress at the time with the 1:300 scale model at Didcot, and these showed that a satisfactory alignment could be arranged without difficulty. A shaft support structure was therefore designed which was in principle a large-diameter flanged pipe, stiffened with external longitudinal and circumferential ribs and provided with feet to

Shaft support structure (courtesy of Davy Cleveland Barrier Consortium)

enable it to be accurately located in the pier. The concrete of the pier would then be cast round it so that the structure was totally embedded in the pier. Accurate location would of course be vital, as once the structure was concreted in, it would be virtually impossible to make any adjustment. In the case of piers with a 61 m gate on each side, a double-ended structure was used. These castings with their reinforcing ribs weighed 125 t. This design provided a totally solid and rigid support for the shafts and solved the problem very satisfactorily.

To complete the design, it was necessary to decide on appropriate architectural treatment for the piers. There was a danger that the structure would look like an unfinished bridge, with the nine piers in the river but no superstructure. The Architect to the GLC was responsible for the architectural treatment, but with his staff working as part of the Consulting Engineer's team. After considering a wide variety of designs, Brian Thaxton, the architect directly in charge of the job, came up with curved housings over the piers, to be clad with stainless steel. Timber proved to be the most suitable material for the structure to receive the stainless steel cladding. The design of the structure was entrusted to the Timber Research and Development Association, and wind tunnel tests were carried out by Bristol University to check the aerodynamics. The timber roofs have a triple skin of European redwood boarding supported by laminated iroko ribs and covered with stainless steel; this is a hard material and the 28 gauge sheets had to be limited to about 600 mm width to allow them to conform with the double curvature of the roof. The strips were joined with standing seams into which clips were folded to secure the sheets to the roof. After initiating the design, Brian Thaxton transferred to the Housing Department of the GLC and was succeeded by Tony Petty.

The evolution of the final design was now almost complete, and the stage had been reached when a contract plan had to be devised to enable the construction to go ahead. For practical reasons, and to enable work to start as soon as possible, it was decided to split the work up into a number of separate contracts. Both the GLC and their Consulting Engineers, Rendel Palmer & Tritton, agreed in principle that these contracts should as far as possible be of moderate size and duration. In the case of the civil engineering work in the piers and sills, it was not considered advisable to split up the work. A large contract of long duration was the inevitable result. Even if this decision is examined with hindsight, it still appears to be the only practical course.

Separate contracts were decided upon for the construction of the gates and machinery. The control tower, generator house, workshop and electricity sub-stations on the north and south banks formed a separate contract, and further contracts were also planned for the generators themselves, switchgear, control panels and services. A number of small contracts were envisaged for specialist items such as the special bearings for the gates, the steel shafts on which the bearings fitted, and the large castings for the shaft support structures. It was planned that the shaft support structures would be supplied to the civil engineering contractor who would be responsible for placing them in the correct position and concreting them in. The shafts, after a trial assembly with the shaft support structure, would be supplied to the gate contractor who would fit them into the gate ends and then make the connection to the shaft support structure when the gate end was placed in position against the pier.

The splitting up of the work on this basis was both logical and practical, but it placed a heavy burden on the Consulting Engineers' site and inspection staff to ensure that all the work was done to the required degree of accuracy. The initial dredging of a diversion channel for shipping to the north of the existing navigational channel and its subsequent maintenance were made separate contracts. A schedule with details of the contracts is given in Appendix 4.

During the summer of 1971 Peter Shallow, who had been Deputy Project Manager from the early days of the GLC investigation, left the team and was replaced by Bill Dickens from the Central Electricity Generating Board.

In parallel with the completion of the design of the structure and the preparation of the contract plan, powers were obtained from Parliament to enable the GLC to construct the barrier. The Solicitor and Parliamentary Officer of the GLC, H. Wilson, advised that the soundest course of action would be to promote a Private Bill in Parliament to get the powers necessary for the construction of the work. Subsequent experience showed the good sense of this advice. The Bill was drafted by Hugh Fulton, the Parliamentary Officer in the Department, and deposited in the autumn of 1971. Objections were lodged, but in general these were overcome by negotiation with those concerned. The Bill reached Committee stage in mid-April 1972. The members of the Committee were David James (Chairman), Ronald Bray, Hugh McCartney, and J.T. Price. Twelve petitions were lodged against the Bill, but in general these were not against the principle, but to ensure that the interests of the Petitioners were safeguarded. The Chairman took great care that everyone got a full and fair hearing. Ray Horner gave evidence for the GLC and the Kent and Essex River Boards were represented by the Chief Engineers, Jim Taylor and Ted Snell. The hearing of evidence took two weeks and the Bill passed its committee stage with minor amendments only. The House of Commons Committee set a precedent by carrying out an inspection of the site by river, as a final stage in the hearing. No special problems arose with the hearing before the House of Lords and the Bill received Royal Assent in August 1972. In practice the competent drafting of the Act has proved a very valuable asset in carrying out the project.

The GLC now had the powers to carry out the work. In order to get something moving on site at an early date, a contract for clearance of the site on the south side of the river was let to H. Smith Ltd of Orpington. Desmond Plummer (now Lord Plummer) struck the first blow by swinging a demolition ball suspended from a crane. This started the demolition of a factory building on the Eastmoor St site. Once the site was cleared, work could go ahead on the first construction contract for building a new section of river wall, constructing access roads, and an office building for the Consulting Engineer's site staff. At the same time contract documents were prepared for the main civil engineering, machinery and gate contracts. Lists of firms who had expressed interest in tendering for the work, and who were considered to have the necessary expertise and resources to carry out such large and important contracts, had been prepared, and the tender documents were dispatched to these organisations in the spring of 1973.

A diversion channel for the vessels using the reach was necessary at an early stage. This had to be dredged in the shallow water to the north of the normal shipping channel as a decision had been taken to build the southern half of the barrier first. In order to maintain the momentum of the project this decision was taken before the results of the Hydraulic Research Station's work on the probable siltation effects in the diversion channel had been carried out. These results when available predicted heavy siltation in the diversion channel, dredging being expected to be at the rate of over a million cubic metres of silt a year to maintain the channel. However, it was then too late to amend all the documents to allow the work to start on the northern side of the river first, without considerable delay and wasted effort. The only practicable course was to adhere to the plan and deal with the siltation if and when it occurred. A contract to allow for maintenance dredging was therefore let so that the channel could be kept open, but the decision to follow the plan was proved right, as the predicted heavy siltation never happened. The wet autumn of 1974, followed by the drought of 1975—76, no doubt played a part in this fortunate state of affairs, as the maximum silt concentrations first moved downriver with the high upland flow, and then upriver as the flow fell away. The steady improvement in the sewage effluents from the Beckton and Crossness works must have helped too. The predictions of siltation in the northern diversion channel had been obtained from the new hydraulic model constructed by the Hydraulics Research Station. The main study area of the new model extended from Lower Pool to Halfway Reach, the river bed being correctly moulded between London Bridge and Crayfordness. Upriver of London Bridge it was represented in the form of a labyrinth, and downriver of Crayfordness as an idealised model entry length of trapezoidal section, designed to produce the correct tidal volume as far as Tilbury Landing Stage. Care was taken to incorporate all major bridges and jetties between Lambeth Bridge and Crayfordness, to simulate the head losses experienced in nature. Tides were generated by a hinged-weir tide generator, controlled by a cam cut to the required profile. Salinities were reproduced in the model by mixing a calculated quantity of brine solution to the tidal storage tank. Current velocities were measured by current meters and current directions by floats with candles attached to sub-surface drogues which were photographed for a timed exposure. Tests carried out included float tracking and current velocity measurements, gate failure studies, and siltation studies of conditions during barrier construction and on completion.

Tests on the second HRS model were not sufficiently advanced for results to be available for the Committee stage of the Barrier Bill. Use was therefore made of a model constructed by the Hydraulics Division of the Wimpey Laboratories for the GLC to investigate the hydraulic effects of the proposed Woolwich River Crossing and the Thamesmead River Wall. The model was constructed to a horizontal scale of 1:300 and a vertical scale of 1:75, and simulated 15 miles of river from the Lower Pool to the western end of Long Reach. Tests were carried out to investigate flow patterns and to compare existing conditions with those when the barrier was in position and during the various stages of construction. These tests proved very useful in giving evidence for the House of Commons Committee and also provided an interesting comparison with the HRS results available later.

10

The civil engineering contract

The construction of the barrier entailed the letting of a number of contracts, the largest being the civil engineering contract (contract 3), which comprised the construction of the north and south abutments, the nine piers in the river with their superstructures and the sills in the bed of the river between the piers. Tenders were invited from five firms or consortia in June 1973. Two of the firms withdrew during the tender period, and three tenders were received in November 1973. The tenders were all heavily qualified in respect of costs of labour, materials, and possible delays. Negotiations had to be entered into to try to arrive at a contract basis which was acceptable to the GLC and the Ministry of Agriculture, Fisheries and Food which had become the Government Department responsible for the project after the passing of the Thames Barrier Act.

These negotiations were difficult and prolonged, and an extension of the six-month validity period of the tenders had to be sought. One firm, Sir Robert McAlpine and Sons Ltd, declined to extend the validity period of their tender. After a further period of negotiation the Acting Director of Public Health Engineering of the GLC, Cliff Darlow, was able to recommend the acceptance of the tender of the Costain Civil Engineering, Tarmac Construction, and Hollandsche Beton Maatschappij BV (CTH) consortium.

In the circumstances, it was not surprising that tenderers were not willing to commit themselves to a large contract lasting 4½–5 years under the normal civil engineering conditions of contract. There had been a period of high inflation, and considerable industrial unrest. At the time of tender there was a restriction on deliveries of oil, an essential item for a construction contract with so many units of mechanical plant powered by diesel engines. Contractors were concerned that work could be delayed through industrial disputes which were in no way related to their particular contract.

The contract was finally signed in July 1974, the main departures from the Standard Conditions being that the Contractor was only responsible for the cost of industrial disputes affecting the whole of the labour force for a total of 21 days in each year. It was agreed at the same time that Contract rates should be reviewed at the end of the first two years in the light of experience to date, and provision was made for termination of the Contract if it were not possible to agree the revised rates. It was also agreed that the Engineer (Rendel Palmer & Tritton) had power to grant an extension of time for delays due to national shortages of materials and disruption due to Government regulations in connection with fuel and power and other matters. Safeguards were also provided for the effects of high rates of inflation. The Contract was signed in July 1974, but the Contractor requested that, in view of the size and complexity of the work, the official starting date should be delayed six months to enable him to assemble plant, obtain materials, and allocate staff. This was agreed and a start with the work on site was made in January 1975, although some preliminary work in setting up plant was carried out before that date.

As already discussed, an essential preliminary to the main civil contract was the dredging of a diversion channel to the north of the central pier to enable shipping to pass the site during the construction of the southern piers. The dredging contract which required the removal of about a million cubic metres of material was let to Kier Broekhoven Ltd. The work started at the end of August 1974 and was complete by the end of February 1975. This contract unfortunately produced the first fatality on the job. A lighterman checking the moorings of one of the spoil barges fell overboard and was drowned. A further contract for the maintenance of the channel was let to the Westminster Dredging Co. The year 1974 saw changes in the GLC's Barrier team with Bill Dickens and Brian Hall leaving and Norman Thurstun becoming Deputy Project Manager and John Holloway Assistant Project Manager. Technical back-up was provided by Eddie Adams and Roger Vine, and Henry Gordon kept a watchful eye on costs. Raymond Grainger took over from Arthur Mascall as the GLC liaison engineer on site. The work in the main civil contract entailed the placing of 400 000 t of concrete and 50 000 t of steel.

The plan agreed with the main contractor was a fairly simple one. Construction was to start from the south side, the piers being built in sequence until the central pier (no. 6) was reached. The piers on the south side were to be founded on the chalk, up to 16 m below river bed level, and built inside steel cofferdams (rectangular boxes constructed of steel sheet piles driven deep into the chalk below the river bed). Access to

Woolwich Reach, January 1975 (courtesy of the Greater London Council)

the piers was to be provided by the construction of a jetty out from the south bank to the site of the central pier. To protect the work from shipping, a central river fender was to be provided, using heavy German Peine H-section piles. Work on the southern piers was expected to take two and a half years, when shipping would be switched to pass between the completed piers and work could go ahead on the northern half. It was proposed that the sills would be constructed in a building area reclaimed from the river bed adjacent to the north shore and a little upriver of the centre line of the barrier. The level of the floor of this area was to be sufficiently below high-water level that the area could be flooded and the completed sills floated out.

Excavation for both the piers and the abutments would have to be carried out under water, and the base of the excavation sealed by a 5 m thick slab of concrete placed under water. Even this thickness of concrete would not be enough to resist the full water pressure expected on the underside of the concrete slab, and holes were to be formed in the slab to enable submersible pumps to pump the water from the underside of the slab and so reduce the uplift water pressure. Work started on site in January 1975 with the construction of the access jetty, and the driving of the bearing piles to support the piling gantry for driving the piles of the cofferdams.

An important decision taken at that stage was to work two twelve-hour shifts for five days a week, with the weekends available for plant maintenance and picking up any slippage which had taken place. This

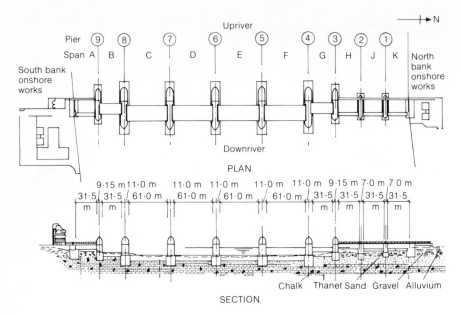

Upriver

→ N

Pier ⑨ ⑧ ⑦ ⑥ ⑤ ④ ③ ② ①

Span A B C D E F G H J K | North bank onshore works

South bank onshore works

Downriver

PLAN

9·15 m 11·0 m   11·0 m 11·0 m   11·0 m 11·0 m 9·15 m 7·0 m 7·0 m

31·5/31·5/61·0 m   61·0 m /61·0 m /61·0 m/31·5/31·5/31·5/31·5
m   m

Chalk   Thanet Sand Gravel Alluvium

SECTION

Site plan

decision was one which was to have important repercussions later. A difficulty involving labour relations arose at an early stage. In the light of the, as then, newly published Merrison Rules the Consulting Engineers considered that the box girders for carrying the piling frame were not strong enough for the loads to be put on them and required stiffening of the webs by welding on angles. The welders claimed a 'plus rate' for work over water. The management resisted this since on a job of this kind the effects could be far reaching. The work was held up and the piling delayed until a compromise solution was reached.

Work continued fairly steadily during 1975, although not up to programme. The decision to work two twelve-hour shifts, although common enough in civil engineering, was not working out well; the carrot of high wages due to the overtime being worked was not buying industrial peace or keeping the job on schedule.

There were two reasons for this. A good deal of the labour was recruited locally in a predominantly industrial area, with a bad level of industrial disputes and a history of redundancies for dock and other workers. Many of the men were used to working a 40-hour week under factory conditions, and the high wages did not compensate for the loss of leisure time. Consequently only a small proportion of the labour force worked a full 60-hour week, quite a number working 40 hours only and most something around 50 hours. This had the effect of reducing productivity by some 20%. In addition the system provided an excellent

Site, summer 1976 (courtesy of the Greater London Council)

bargaining ploy in any dispute over bonus levels, as lack of satisfaction by the workforce with levels fixed could be expressed by banning over-time. This immediately reduced progress to about 60% of what could be achieved.

Technical difficulties were also encountered. Driving the sheet piles for the cofferdams into the chalk was difficult. These piles had to be driven down well below the founding level for the piers to give them a good 'bite' into the chalk to resist the water pressure. The use of the Larssen no. 6 pile, the heaviest available from UK sources, entailed very heavy cross strutting to resist the loads due to water pressure. Four 'frames' consisting of heavy longitudinal girders with cross struts had to be used, as the depth from the top of the piles to the base of the excavation was about 30 m. The top frame only could be placed 'in the dry', the remainder having to be placed under water. The heavy strutting made excavation under water very difficult, and special grabs had to be used. A Japanese rock drill was tried, but it did not like the flints in the chalk. Levelling and cleaning up the bottom for the concrete caused problems as river silt was deposited in the cofferdams on every tide. Special air lift pumps were developed to overcome this problem. The basis of the pump is a vertical steel tube. Air is blown into the base of the tube which is lowered into the water until the bottom of the tube is about a foot above the surface being excavated. The air rising up the tube reduces the density of the air/water mixture in the tube, and so the water pressure at the base forces the air/water column up the tube with considerable force. This in turn induces a rush of water into the bottom of the tube with such velocity that even hard chalk can be eroded. These pumps were most effective in the cleaning up and final levelling of the bottom of the excavation, but could do little about the material immediately below the heavy longitudinal beams that were part of the strutting frames. Special offset grabs were tried, but finally small explosive charges placed by divers had to be used to remove chalk wedged in the troughs of the Larssen piles. It was essential to remove this material, since water could blow up past the concrete slab when the water was pumped out of the cofferdam if this material were left in place.

At last a satisfactory result was achieved and the pouring of the concrete under water for the base slab could go ahead. The first pour was on

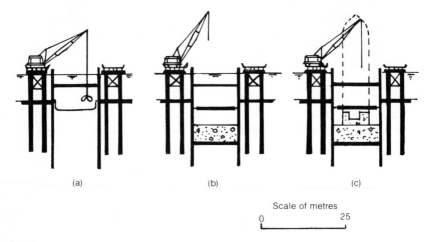

(a)   (b)   (c)

Scale of metres

0   25

Stages in cofferdam construction

98

Cofferdam after dewatering

pier 9 in the summer of 1976 which was ready before the south abutment (the piers are numbered from the north). The successful completion of this operation was quite a milestone in the progress of the job, as it was a vital step in the overall plan for pier construction. To avoid the cement being washed out of the concrete during the placing operation, the concrete was fed down 300 mm dia. vertical pipes called 'tremie pipes'. The concrete flowed out of these pipes and spread across the floor of the excavation. As far as possible the lower ends of the pipes had to be kept submerged in the mass of concrete already placed. By later standards the first pour was a fairly small one, 7000 t, but this was still a lot of con-

Aerial view of the north bank dry dock (courtesy of the Greater London Council)

crete. Cores cut from the hardened slab showed that an almost perfect joint had been made with the undisturbed chalk underlying the site. This was a considerable achievement and reflected great credit on the engineer's Representative on site, George Davies, his Deputy, Tony Hepplewhite, and the Assistant Engineer's Representative, John Hounslow, the inspection team and the Contractor's engineers and labour force. The pour took five days of continuous work round the clock. To keep the concrete plastic during the operation, a retarder was added in the mix. A cube strength of $15 \, \text{N/mm}^2$ at 56 days with a maximum cementitious content of $450 \, \text{kg/m}^3$ was specified. A pulverised fuel ash content of 50% of the cementitious content was used to reduce the heat evolved in the setting process.

Meanwhile work was going ahead on the north bank with the reclamation of an area of shallow water to provide the building site for the sills which later would be placed between each of piers 3—9. The first step was to isolate the area from the river by driving steel sheet piles to form a wall on three sides of a rectangle 145 m by 120 m, the fourth side being the north bank of the river. Before closure of the dam, as much silt as possible was dredged out of the enclosed area. Once the area was sealed off, a well point dewatering system was installed to dry the area out. The floor was excavated to the required depth and sea-dredged ballast tipped and levelled to form a base for concrete slabs which were laid down to form the working area. In the first phase of the work, two large sills, 60 m by 27 m, and two small sills, 31 m by 20 m, were constructed. Crane rails were laid in the floor slab to enable tower cranes to be used to service the construction site; and an access ramp was built to allow lorry access to the area.

Working conditions in the north bank dry dock were those of a normal construction site and progress here was much better than in the confined conditions of the pier cofferdams. This posed a problem, since the sills could not be placed in position until the piers were complete and the cofferdam piling removed. Construction would therefore have to be slowed down unless time lost on the piers could be made up. This seemed unlikely so some diversion of resources took place. Possible storage sites for the completed sills were investigated, and the Royal Docks were finally selected.

By mid-summer 1976, the time for the Review of the main civil contract had arrived. The GLC was far from happy about the progress of the work. The temporary works for the southern half of the river were virtually complete, and at long last the first underwater pour of concrete in pier 9 cofferdam was about to take place. In the first eighteen months of work, the job was six months behind programme. Unless drastic steps were taken to improve organisation and productivity, it would require seven years to complete the work, and the barrier would not be operable until the flood season of 1981—82.

The GLC's dissatisfaction with this situation was made abundantly clear at the start of the Review negotiations by the then Controller of Operational Services Cyril Whitehouse, the Director of Public Health Engineering, Derek Ayres, and the Consulting Engineers, Rendel Palmer & Tritton, represented by Peter Cox. Termination of the Contract was given serious consideration, but was not really a viable course on grounds of delay and cost. In addition there was always the possibility that any new organisation would experience the same learning phase as the CTH Consortium. Review negotiations were prolonged and detailed and were not completed until the late autumn of 1976. It was finally agreed that the Contractor was paid his net audited costs for the first two years, a revision of contract rates by some 16% for future work, agreement on a lump sum to cover the cost of industrial disputes for the two years up to the summer of 1978, and limitation of profit and loss clauses. The agreement on net cost for the first two years was very reasonable on both sides, the Contractor did not have to carry forward a loss, and the Client got 25% of the work (based on the figure for value of measured work) for £15 million at mid-1976 prices. Simple arithmetic suggests that it should have been possible to complete the civil contract for £60 million plus post-1976 inflation. Alas, in practice these things are not quite so simple.

The sting was in the tail, the limitation-of-loss clause, since the Contractor never managed to make a profit, in spite of contract rates being enhanced by some 16%. This in effect converted the contract to a cost-plus basis, and it can be argued that a full revision to a target cost contract at that stage would, with hindsight, have been wise. This course was advocated by the Chief Engineer of MAFF, at that time Gordon Cole, but was not favoured by the administrators or the Treasury. The background to this may have been some Government contracts at the time where contractors had made excessive profits, and the main object on the Treasury side seemed to be to ensure this did not happen on the barrier contract! The GLC Treasurers were also very suspicious of any unorthodox contract after the unfortunate experience of the 'Value—Cost' contract for buildings at Thamesmead. In the circumstances, the climate was not yet right for this step to be taken. The main benefit of the Review was the reorganisation of top management carried out by the CTH Consortium. John Grice was appointed Project Manager and John Reeve became more closely involved with the job. John Grice brought an entirely new spirit to the site, instead of putting the emphasis on costs (in fairness contractors do have to worry about costs), he concentrated on getting the job done. If productivity was low on the night shift during a spell of cold weather in February, he was out on site in the early hours of the morning to see what could be done about it. Such action is worth several tons of computer-aided management monitoring data, which after all only tells the man on the site with any sort of feel for the job what he knows already. This is a most unfashionable statement but it is true all the same. There may appear to be substitutes for doing things the hard way, but they often prove to be of little value when tested in the harsh climate of actual achievement. Cosy conferences in warm offices may help to get the work done, but they will achieve little if not backed up by a good look at what is actually happening at the work face.

The new team quickly realised the weakness of the two 12-hour shifts to achieve 24-hour working. Introduction of three 8-hour shifts was proposed, and gained immediate approval of the GLC, MAFF, the Consulting Engineers and the Unions, the latter as it would lead to at least a 50% increase of the labour force. There was considerable local unemployment and this was seen as a positive step in helping to alleviate the situation. Unfortunately the site labour did not take such a utopian view. They saw a considerable loss of overtime earnings and a smaller pay packet at the end of the week. The negotiations to achieve the three-shift working were long and frustrating. In the end agreement could not be reached, even with the carrot of a very generous shift allowance, and generally management bending backwards to achieve agreement. The only course was to impose the three-shift working which the management was entitled to do, under the terms of the civil engineering working rule agreement. The inevitable result occurred, an all-out stoppage by the Contract 3 labour force. The strike lasted two months from early May to the beginning of July. Finally agreement was reached on the three eight-hour shifts and work was resumed. There was, however, a feeling of resentment by the labour force, and the proposal to add half an hour overtime per shift for handover between teams was not accepted. This was a considerable handicap and the problem was not solved until the 1979 agreement on bonus payments. Progress.in the six months prior to the strike had been quite good, all the remaining underwater pours having been completed on the southern piers, except pier 7.

Pier 7, however, proved to be a problem. The underwater concrete pour was carried out in November 1977, and dewatering of the cofferdam was put in hand. As the water level fell, uplift pressure under the slab built up, in spite of pumping from the pressure relief wells. Reluctantly the decision was taken to reflood the cofferdam as otherwise there was the danger that the 14 000 t plug might be pushed up like a cork out of a bottle. Analysis of the pattern of the build-up of the uplift pressure pointed to water leaking past damaged clutches in the piling or else finding its way through fissures in the chalk. In either case the remedy was the same—to seal up the leak by grouting up the area of the river bed adjacent to the point of weakness. This work was put in hand, but took time. As a result, work on this pier was five months behind programme when the cofferdam was finally dewatered.

By the end of 1977 the four sills in the north cofferdam were virtually complete, and the foundations for pier 2 and the north abutment were in hand. Work could not start on the foundation to pier 1 as the site was obstructed by one of the small sills, but commenced as soon as the first four sills had been floated out and the dry dock restored. These piers were founded on the Thanet Sand, as in this area the chalk lies at a depth of over 20 m. The Thanet Sand is very firm if confined, but can become a quicksand if exposed to a current of water. Care had to be taken that the exposed surface of the sand was quickly sealed with the underwater concrete pour as soon as the formation was ready.

A sub-contract had been let to Tysons of Liverpool for the construction of the roofs to the piers. It was planned to construct the roofs in a number of sections which could be erected on the piers by floating crane with a minimum of work in the exposed river situation. By the end of 1977 the fabrication of the roof for pier 9 was complete apart from a little work on the stainless steel sheeting. An interesting problem arose with the sheeting of these roofs. The stainless steel sheets had to be in fairly narrow strips to lie satisfactorily on the curved timber skin. The sheets had to be joined by turning the edge of one sheet up and folding the edge of the next sheet over it. The direction of fold had to be such that the water running down the roof would not leak through the joint. On one side of the roof it was alleged that this could be done normally by a right-handed plumber, but on the other side it was necessary either to employ left-handed plumbers or to persuade the plumbers to work upside down. Fortunately it appeared that Tysons were able to recruit enough left-handed plumbers to get the job done on programme. As it happened, due to the delay with the pier construction, the roof sections had to be stored until the piers were sufficiently advanced for erection of the roofs to go ahead.

By late summer 1978, work on the two large sills and the two smaller sills in the north bank dry dock was sufficiently far advanced for the dock to be flooded, a gap to be formed in the surrounding steel sheet-piled wall, and the sills to be floated out. They were moored temporarily upriver of the site, but subsequently were transferred to the Royal Docks as a safer anchorage. On 12 January 1978, an event occurred which caused considerable anxiety. A storm surge caused a high water at London Bridge which was less than 1 ft below the highest recorded level, that of 1953. Water rose so high outside the barrier cofferdams that water poured through the holes drilled in the piles for handling. The level which had been fixed by the main contractor on a calculated risk basis, was that of the 1953 high water of 5.20 m above OD(N) (approximately mean sea level.) After that night the 'calculated risk' did not look quite so good. The cofferdams were hastily raised by 0.5 m. The impact of this tide spread much further upriver, to the Houses of Parliament. The Minister of Agriculture, Fisheries and Food himself expressed concern over barrier progress and requested informally if barrier completion could be expedited, even at the risk of spending a little more money. This initiative was enthusiastically taken up by the GLC. A study of methods of making the barrier operable at an early date was put in hand.

After reviewing the possibilities, it was evident that the most practical method was one which had been worked out previously, but put in cold storage as it was not thought to be feasible from the navigation aspect. This proposal would entail the reduction of the two 61 m openings requested by the PLA for navigation in the second phase of barrier construction to a single 40 m opening. In the light of events it seemed that there was a good chance of getting this proposal accepted. The initial approach to the PLA brought rejection of the single 40 m opening proposal, but gained the concession that a single 61 m opening could be accepted provided a traffic study showed that there would not be unacceptable delays to shipping. The study was undertaken and showed that the worst delay should not exceed half an hour, which was considered acceptable. A revised study on the engineering aspect showed that whereas there was a potential saving of a year and a half with the 40 m opening, a 61 m opening would allow a year to be saved in the period of time necessary to get the barrier operating. This seemed well worthwhile, although it was appreciated that additional resources would be necessary, and this would entail additional cost. This plan received general acceptance and was a major factor in the renegotiations which were in hand with the CTH Consortium, since the two-year period covered by the 1976 agreement was now running out. To end an eventful year, a 7000 t Greek ship went off course and ran into the north bank dry dock on 11 November. The damage due to the ship going off course was fairly easily rectified. It appeared that she was coming downriver and ran into a patch of fog. Turning from Bugsby's into Woolwich Reach, she did not alter course soon enough and hit the north cofferdam at a point where there was a double skin of sheet piling for an unloading bay. The bow buckled the outer sheet piles, but did not penetrate the inner row. This was fortunate, as there was only a slight risk that the following high water would burst through the inner skin and flood the reclaimed area. Remedial works were put in hand at once and all was well.

On New Year's Eve 1978 a surge tide, only eight inches lower than the 1953 tide at London Bridge, reinforced everyone's resolve to make the barrier operable as soon as possible. Agreement had been reached with the PLA and shipping interests on the single 61 m opening and it was now necessary to sort out with the contractors the way in which the modified programme could be financed.

It was accepted by both the GLC and Government that the main civil contractor must have a reasonable financial carrot to put in a big effort to finish the job. The organisations involved were tying up a considerable proportion of skilled manpower and plant on a project which, although not making a loss (the provisions of the 1976 agreement saw to that), was not earning the kind of profit which those resources could earn elsewhere. The solution to this problem was to renegotiate the contract providing for bonuses for completion on time and within a target cost. The object of the negotiations was to arrive at figures which supplied the incentive without too lavish expenditure of public money. In this exercise the GLC, meeting only 25% of the cost, tended to be rather more generous than the Government, which was meeting 75% of the cost! Negotiations were prolonged and detailed. As the authority responsible for the construction of the barrier, the GLC took the lead, represented by the Chairman of the Public Services Committee, Bernard Brook-Partridge, supported by the Controller of Operational Services, Laurence Peterken, the Director of Public Health Engineering, Derek Ayres and his staff. The MAFF team was led by Alan Longworth (Under

Secretary) and the Chief Engineer, Gordon Cole, with his team of engineers and administrators. The agreement which emerged was criticised as being too generous, but it achieved its object of getting the job done, which was what really mattered.

The main element of the agreement was a target cost of £165 million with the provision of sharing profits or losses if the cost was either 5% less or 5% more than the target figure. A limit of £12 million was put on both the profit or loss figure to be shared. A sliding scale of bonuses was agreed as the incentive for finishing on time. The object was to get the barrier operable by the flood season 1982—83. The target-cost figure applied to expenditure incurred after 1 January 1979 and was index linked to allow for inflation.

Towards the end of 1978, the Ministry of Agriculture, Fisheries and Food approached the GLC with the proposal that a three-man advisory team should be set up to advise the Minister on how progress with the work could be best maintained and improved so as to ensure prompt completion of the work without undue escalation of cost. The team consisted of Urquhart Broadbent who had been a Director of John Laing and Son Ltd, a firm with long experience with large construction projects, Irving Johnstone, a senior engineer with Imperial Chemical Industries with considerable experience of acting for the Client in major engineering projects, and Bert Ray of the Transport and General Workers Union to advise on labour relations. Having made themselves familiar with the project and the problems involved, the team came up with a number of suggestions and provided a useful independent group to give an objective assessment of the various difficulties which arose from time to time.

Agreement with the PLA on the reduced width of channel for shipping enabled work to go ahead right away on the cofferdam for pier 3, the pier in the shallow water on the north side of the diversion channel. Following the experience with the southern piers and the difficulties with excavation, a modified design was used for the three northern cofferdams, for piers 3—5. For the outer wall it was proposed to use a much heavier H-section pile available from West Germany, known as the Peine pile, which had already been used in the mid-river fender. These piles were driven in pairs with the webs at right angles to the centre line of the cofferdam wall. The gaps between the flanges, which formed a smooth continuous outer and inner face, were sealed by a special linking bar. The piles were dropped into prebored holes in the substratum, which were filled with a bentonite slurry. The piles were then driven for about 6 m into the Thanet Sand or Chalk. As a result the wall had sufficient strength to permit the main excavation to be carried out before any cross strutting was in position. Furthermore only a single frame consisting of walings and cross struts was necessary to resist the full water

106

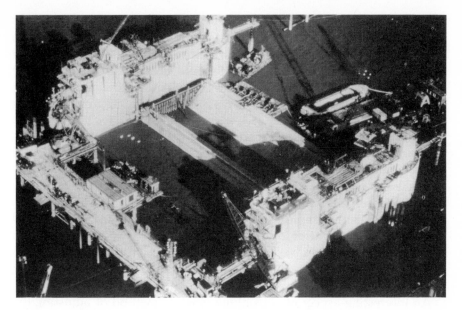

Placing the sill, 61 m opening (courtesy of Aero Industrial Photographic)

pressure when the water was pumped out of the cofferdam. The cost was heavy in terms of the quantity of steel required. Each pair of piles weighed 20 t, and 120 pairs of piles were needed to complete the perimeter of one of the larger cofferdams, over 2400 t of steel! The advantages of access for excavation and pier construction were very great, and the work on these northern piers went ahead very quickly.

Access to the site of pier 5, the critical pier which would control the date for completing the civil engineering and, in turn, the date on which the barrier could become operable, was dependent on being able to switch river traffic from the northern diversion channel. This in turn depended on the removal of the cofferdams from piers 6 and 7, the selected opening being between these piers. This was achieved on 16 June 1979 and the placing of the first sill, the 31.5 m sill between piers 8 and 9 followed soon after on 5 September. Clearances between the piers for placing these sills were very small, approximately 50 mm at each end. This first sill-placing operation was a milestone, and everyone felt more confident when the operation was successfully accomplished. The sills were floated into position between the piers and secured by cables controlled by winches. Heavy suspension cables were then attached to special posts provided at the four corners of the sill. The cables were fed out by specially modified Freyssinet post-tensioning jacks. Water was then pumped into the gate recess scallop of the sill which lost buoyancy and became suspended from the cables. When fully flooded the load on the cables was about 400 t for one of the large sills. It was then vital that lowering of the sill should take place faster than the fall in the tide, as this operation normally took place on a falling tide. Since even the 31.5 m sill had a total weight of 4000 t, the sill could become suspended on the cables with disastrous results. The alternative method would have been to float in at low water, with restricted manoeuvrability of the vessels involved. Another possibility was that the sill could have been allowed to fall freely with the tide, but then in the event of some obstruction causing one end to be held up, there would be no control and the sill could have jammed between the piers. The placing of the first 31.5 m sill was only the prelude to placing (the use of the term 'sinking' was definitely discouraged on site) of the first 61 m sill in October. Both operations went through with complete success due to careful preparation and good planning of the operation by the CTH team. There was some vibration of the lowering cables during the first operation, but this was traced to the control system for keeping the sill level during the operation being too sensitive and was corrected for the second operation.

An interesting aspect of sill sinking was the method of adjusting the level of the sills on the supporting plinths on the piers. Special jacks were installed on the piers for the sill to 'land' on. These jacks were in pairs, a pair for each corner of the sill. The jacks are circular pads of steel about 1 m in diameter, each pad being made of two thin discs of steel sealed round the edges. Provision is made to pump a liquid resin at high pressure into the small space between the discs. As the liquid forces the discs apart, the jack will lift anything placed on it. These jacks have only a limited travel but a large load capacity. When the sill was lowered on to the jacks a check was made of the level and the jacks were pumped up to position the sill correctly. When checking the sill for position, use was made of the twin access tunnels provided in the sills to position a telescope on the pier sealed against the entry of water to observe a grid of lines marked on an illuminated target disc fixed in the tunnel opening in the sill. As the sill was lowered into position the grid was observed and corrections made to ensure the sill was correctly placed.

Overall, things went well in 1979. In May an agreement, referred to as the Site Supplemental Agreement, had been signed between the CTH management and the Unions representing the workforce to achieve good working relationships and to avoid industrial disputes for the duration of the civil contract. Provided this was achieved, payments would be made to each member of the workforce on site of £500 for each of seven stages in the completion of the work. At each stage other than the first, a proportion of the labour force became redundant and had to leave the site. This agreement proved to be very successful and labour relations improved to a marked degree. (Perhaps an effort should have been made earlier to adopt this course of action, although the climate might not have been right.)

So 1980 started in a much better situation than had appeared likely in January 1979. Things continued to go well during the year, the last concrete underwater pour for pier 5 having been placed by mid summer. By the end of the year piers 1—3 and the north abutment were complete apart from some minor works.

In 1981 navigation was switched from the 61 m opening between piers 6 and 7 to the opening between piers 7 and 8. This was a hard decision as work on placing the gate ends by the mechanical and gate contractor was not complete, and had to be delayed a year to allow the civil contractor to get on with his part of the job. Subsequent events proved this to have been the right decision. The 61 m sill for the opening between piers 6 and 7 was placed in position on 20 March 1981. Progress on piers 3—5 was good, and the last structural concrete in a main pier structure was placed in position on 8 June. Once the structural concrete of the piers was complete there remained the difficult problem of the removal of the cofferdams, the steel cocoon in which the pier had been built. The section of the heavy piles below river bed level had to be left in place as part of the pier foundation, but the portion above had to be taken away. In the case of the earlier cofferdams with the Larssen piles this had been difficult enough, but with the Peine piles with the double skin this was a much greater problem. The PLA required the piles to be cut off 1 m below river bed level, to avoid any risk of scour uncovering the pile stump. This meant that it was really only practical to cut the piles from the inside of the cofferdam. It was therefore necessary to cut a hole in the inner face to allow access to cut the outer skin. This would have to be done before the cofferdam was flooded, so the thrust of the water pressure would have to be carried during and after the operation. The solution was to cut the piles with an oxygen lance, and to step the cut through adjacent pairs of piles, one pair being cut at the specified highest level, and the next pair at the lower level. A complete cut could thus be made round the whole perimeter of the cofferdam, but it would still be stable due to the interlocking of the piles. The cofferdam could then be flooded, the struts removed and the sections of the piles above the cut-off level pulled out.

After this system had been devised and one Peine pile cofferdam had been removed, all major operations had been carried out at least once. It was then largely a question of repeat performances to carry the job through to conclusion. The last sill was placed in position on 1 October 1981, and installation of the stainless steel roofs went ahead steadily as access could be provided to the individual piers. The various key dates were met and stage payments made to the workforce, including the final key date for completion of the civil engineering works. John Grice handed over as Project Manager of the CTH Joint Venture to Adrian Franklin who maintained momentum well during the difficult final stages of the contract. The Convenor Steward, Bruce Birdsell, made a major contribution to the successful completion. The run-down of the workforce kept in step with the programme. Bed protection works and the removal of temporary works went ahead as planned. Total cost was well below the agreed target cost and the maximum bonus was earnt.

The heat and burden of getting the gates and machinery installed and working to achieve barrier operability now fell on the Davy Cleveland Barrier Consortium, whose section of the project is described in the next chapter.

11

Gate and machinery contracts

Documents were prepared and issued on the basis of two separate contracts for these sections of the work. DCBC was awarded the contract for the steel gates in July 1974, and after careful evaluation of the tenders submitted for the operating machinery contract, it was decided to award this contract to DCBC as well on the basis of negotiating a merger of the terms governing the two contracts. This was considered to have a number of advantages in reduction of contract price and achievement of good co-ordination of gate and machinery erection. Complications arose over key dates for completion of certain sections of the work and also with responsibilities for delays. The starting date for the machinery contract was October 1974. The Consortium planned to manufacture the machinery at the Davy Loewy works at Sheffield, whereas the gate manufacture would be carried out at the Cleveland Bridge works at Darlington, the gates being assembled at Port Clarence on the north bank of the River Tees.

The Consulting Engineers required the gates to be constructed to a high standard of accuracy to ensure that they could be attached to the gate ends on site without difficulty and to achieve the required clearances for machinery. It was also important that the method of construction used would not lead to high residual stresses in the completed structure. As a result of discussions between the Consulting Engineers and the contractors, the gates were constructed as a number of strips running from end to end. Two edge strips and three intermediate strips suited the arrangement of internal stiffening diaphragms and were also convenient in themselves. The plan was to manufacture as much of the gates as possible at the Darlington works of Cleveland Bridge and to transport the sections by road for assembly at Port Clarence, a distance of about 20 miles. By dividing each strip into four sections, units about

Fabrication of gate sections at Darlington (courtesy of Davy Cleveland Barrier Consortium)

6 m long, 2 m wide and up to 5.3 m high, weighing up to 50 t were produced. These were the largest which could be transported by road without exceptional arrangements. The gate arms were divided up into sections in a similar manner. Fabrication at Darlington started early in 1975 and assembly at Port Clarence later in the year.

The transport of the first section of gate from Darlington to Port Clarence was not without incident, however. The section left Darlington on schedule, mounted on its special heavy transport vehicle, but did not arrive at Port Clarence at the expected time. After an hour had elapsed, staff at Port Clarence began to get rather concerned, although it was rather difficult to imagine how a 50 t section of steel fabrication could be mislaid on a journey of 20 miles! A search party was sent out to locate the missing section. Alas, in spite of careful routeing and police escort, a wrong turning had been taken and the special heavy transport vehicle had got into a housing estate and it was proving very difficult to extricate it. Patience and some careful manoeuvring accomplished this feat and all was well. (The best laid schemes o' mice an' men gang aft a-gley.)

By the end of the year construction of the first gate was well advanced. The construction site at Port Clarence looked impressive with sections of gate and gate ends in various stages of construction. By the summer of 1977 the first gate was nearly complete, but it was to be three years before it would be on its way down to the Thames and erection on the

Gate erection at Port Clarence (courtesy of Davy Cleveland Barrier Consortium)

barrier site. Delays on the civil engineering contract were starting to cause problems and completed gates would have to be stored, either on the Tees or on the Thames until work on the piers was sufficiently advanced to allow gate erection to go ahead. As it happened Cleveland Bridge had urgent work on other contracts and they chose to transfer resources of labour and plant off the manufacture of the barrier gates.

The gates were constructed with the curved surface upwards as this was convenient for the building site and also suited the erection proposals. It would have been a very difficult operation to turn the gate over if this had been necessary to suit the erection plan. The width of the gate (20 m) meant that this could only be done in the deeper part of the North Sea. The decision to build up the gate as a number of longitudinal strips had an influence on the shape: it would have been costly to bend plates to a curve; it was more economical to form the curved surface with a series of narrow flat strips, which was not detrimental to performance as a structure.

The benefits of the four main gates being the same dimensions became apparent once work at Port Clarence got into its stride. The advantages of repetition were even greater on the eight gate ends. Production at Port Clarence generally went along fairly smoothly although there was a bit of excitement over the first gate which finished up about 20 mm short. The shrinkage resulting from the welding together of the sections had been underestimated. It was decided that this difference, an error of

0.03% of the length, could be accommodated fairly easily by the appropriate positioning in pier 8 of the trunnion shaft support structure on which the north gate end was to be mounted, but which had not yet been installed in the pier. For the remaining gates a more generous allowance was made for shrinkage and the required tolerances on overall length were met. The gate ends had to have about 450 t of cast iron balance weights inserted to balance the weight of the gate leaf. For the eight gate ends this added up to 3600 t, quite a handling problem. A special machine was devised to push the cast iron blocks into position in the cellular gate end. They were then grouted in place with a special epoxy resin. The handling problems of gate end erection would have been of considerably less magnitude if the balance weights could have been placed after the gate end had been put in position at site, but this was not really practical. To enable the gate end to rotate on the shafts attached to the shaft support structures built into the piers, large bearings (described later) manufactured by Merrimans of Boston, USA, had to be fitted to the centre of the gate end. To accommodate this, a large steel casting weighing 60 t had to be welded into the centre of each gate end. Before the gate ends were dispatched to the Thames, the bearings and shafts were fitted so the unit was ready to be swung into position and the shaft bolted to the shaft support structure already built into the pier.

Work was going ahead steadily on the machinery at Sheffield and many other places where sub-contracts had been placed. The hydraulic

Gate end centre casting (courtesy of Davy Cleveland Barrier Consortium)

Gate end complete with bearings and shaft (courtesy of Davy Cleveland Barrier Consortium)

cylinders were manufactured by Henry Berry of Leeds and the electrically driven hydraulic pumps by Vickers Hydraulics of Swindon. The hydraulic cylinders for the 61 m gates were very large units, 1100 mm bore and 3130 mm stroke. When supplied with oil at 16.6 N/mm² pressure these cylinders exert a force of over 1500 t. This would produce a pull (or push) on the link connected to the gate arm of over 600 t. The cylinders were manufactured to a high degree of accuracy, the bores being honed to 0.0025 mm. Each of the power packs for the main 61 m gates has three motors and pumps. The main pump is of the swashplate type with a constant power output and is driven by a 140 kW motor; it is either able to produce a small volume of oil at high pressure or a larger volume of oil at a lower pressure. Oil is fed to the main pump by a second pump driven by a 22 kW motor. In addition a pump driven by a 2.5 kW motor provides servo pressure for control purposes.

The locking mechanism for holding the gates firmly in position at the selected point of travel, officially termed the 'shift and latch mechanism' is not of such robust proportions but is much more complex in design. The basis of the device is an arm provided with swinging links which enable it to latch on to a selected pin on the periphery of the gate end. The arm of the mechanism can be moved a short distance, some 6.3 m to adjust the gate position as the inboard end is attached to a pair of bronze nuts mounted on threaded shafts which can be rotated by hydraulic

Hydraulic cylinders (courtesy of Davy Cleveland Barrier Consortium)

Shift and latch mechanism (courtesy of Davy Cleveland Barrier Consortium)

Loading the gate leaf at Port Clarence (courtesy of Davy Cleveland Barrier Consortium)

motors. The machining of these shafts to the required degree of accuracy proved quite difficult due to the spring of the long shaft against the cutting tool. The toggle mechanism which enables the swinging links to clamp on to the pins on the gate arm is rather complicated, and it was considered advisable to manufacture a test rig to try the design out before manufacturing the actual mechanism. No serious snag arose, however, and the mechanisms were to operate satisfactorily in practice.

Due to the delay of the civil contract, most of the machinery items were ready long before they could be installed on site. It was therefore necessary to arrange storage until they could be accepted on site. In the case of the hydraulic pumps provision had to be made for their running periodically to prevent deterioration. Access to site was possible in June 1980, and work went ahead with sufficient speed to enable the first 31.5 m gate and gate end to be put in position by the end of the year. The gates and gate ends were transported to the Thames on specially chartered 6000 t capacity barges. They were loaded by jacking them up and moving six special multi-wheeled bogies underneath. The whole unit was then carefully winched aboard the barge. To allow for varying tide levels and for the effect of the load on the draught of the barge, water ballast equal to the weight of the load was pumped into the barge. As the load was winched slowly aboard, water ballast was pumped out so that the barge remained level with the loading wharf. As an insurance against the load running away, two heavy tractors were connected to the shore

Heavy-lift cranes lifting gate end (courtesy of Davy Cleveland Barrier Consortium)

end of the load. The bogies had over 600 wheels in total and, as each wheel was capable of carrying a 4 t load, there was ample capacity to handle a 1200 t or 1500 t load. The gate ends were loaded in the horizontal position with the bolting flange of the main shaft uppermost.

On arrival at site in the Thames, the gate ends had to be lifted off the barge. It had been decided to use heavy-lift floating cranes supplied by Neptun of Hamburg for this job, and two 800 t cranes working in tandem were necessary to cope with the 1200 t gate end. The plan was to lift the gate end using a special spreader beam and links, and then to turn the end to within 4° of the vertical. This cant was to ensure that the lower part of the gate end circumference when placed against the pier would fit snugly against the seating. It would have been disastrous if the bottom of the gate end had slid out and off the seating on the pier. When placed in position on the pier, the gate end rested on two sets of hydraulic jacks set in seatings in the pier and aligned radially on the centre line of the main shaft about which the gate would rotate. The intention was to use the jacks working together to raise or lower the gate end or, operating in opposite directions, to move it sideways. By this means it was expected that the gate end could be manoeuvred precisely into position—within 1.5 mm—to allow the bolts securing the shaft to the shaft support structure to be fitted. Before any attempt to align the gate took place, however, it was necessary to move it into the vertical since initially it was leaning out at an angle of 4°. This was done by attaching arms to the

118

Gate end in position on pier (courtesy of Davy Cleveland Barrier Consortium)

gate end which were attached to the pier with a hydraulic mechanism which enabled them to be retracted and so pull the gate end into the vertical position.

In the case of the 31.5 m gate the placing of the two 300 t gate ends went according to plan. The first 61 m gate end, 1200 t in weight, was placed successfully on pier 8, but the initial attempt to place the second 61 m gate end on pier 7 failed. When it was lowered on to the jacks, the end rotated and it was not possible to connect the links to enable it to be brought into the vertical position. With hindsight it is apparent that the gate end had not been positioned with sufficient accuracy, since any error in position would be doubled as the gate end came to rest on the second jack unit. A weakness in the plan had been revealed—it was not practical to position the two heavy-lift cranes with their 1200 t load in the tidal current with the degree of accuracy necessary for the success of the operation every time. The operation had to be abandoned and another attempt made a day later. Due to a mischance the second operation also failed—a slight miscalculation on the part of one of the crane operators, or a chance swell in the river, resulted in the 1200 t gate end landing heavily on one jack assembly and the special jack head, necessary to allow the jack to tilt through 4°, fractured. It had to be replaced before a further attempt to get the gate end into position could be undertaken. However, the heavy-lift cranes had another assignment and had to leave the site. In addition it was necessary to switch navigation into the channel between piers 7 and 8 to allow the civil engineering contractors (CTH) to get on with placing the sill between piers 6 and 7. Delay on that operation would affect the whole programme and would delay access for placing gate ends and gates in the other openings, and this in turn would delay the vital date when the barrier could become operational. On the other hand, even though the placing of the gate which was already on site, would be delayed nearly a year, it would be possible to rearrange the programme for placing of the gate for the span between piers 7 and 8 without delaying the date when the barrier would be operable. A break in gate installation would also give time for a rethink of the method to be used to reduce the risk of failure. This was a hard decision to take, but was proved right by subsequent events. As a result of the experience gained it was decided to set the hydraulic jacks vertically so that the initial placing of the gate was not so critical, although this entailed welding lugs on the gate arm to provide the horizontal surface for the jacks to lift against. The new method proved completely successful and when the time came to put the remaining rising sector gates in position, every operation went through without any snags. The gate leaf for the span between piers 7 and 8, already on site, was put into storage in the Royal Docks. Work of course could go ahead on installing the machinery—hydraulic cylinders, crossheads, links, etc., as access was available with the progress of the civil engineering work. A problem arose with the large subframes for the main hydraulic cylinders. These are 12 m long and weigh about 37 t. They are held down by 44 × 40 mm dia. Macalloy bars. The space between the subframes and the concrete bed varied between 18 mm and 110 mm. Tightening down on packs of 'shims' proved unsatisfactory. A simple and more accurate system was adopted, the frames being adjusted to the required level, and then the space between the underside of the frame and the concrete was filled with a special epoxy grout. After the grout had cured, the jacks were removed and the holding-down bolts tightened in a preferred sequence to the specified prestress. No measurable deflection of the subframe was induced by the prestress, irrespective of the thickness of the grout.

The delay was also of advantage in sorting out a tricky problem. At the design stage stainless steel bolts were considered the best choice for connecting the gates to the gate end. Second thoughts suggested that Monel bolts would be more satisfactory. When the bolts and nuts had been delivered, it was discovered that the nuts were of much softer alloy than the bolts to avoid the problem of cold welding of the nut to the bolt. It was then thought that due to progressive shear of the threads of the nut, the required strength would not be achieved. This was quite a serious problem as about 10 000 bolts (studs with nuts each end) and

20 000 nuts were involved. The simple solution of putting two nuts on each end of the stud instead of one was not considered to be effective, as the progressive shear would shear the first nut and then the second. A series of tests were carried out in the Imperial College laboratory to check the strength of the bolted joint. All was well, the tests showing that two nuts would give the required strength. Due to the use of a 'V' thread, stress on the nut caused a radial expansion of the nuts as well as compressive strain. Redistribution of the load took place and the second nut carried its share of the load. A special technique for tightening the nuts was developed to ensure that this took place.

Another problem now came over the horizon. The gate ends for the span between piers 6 and 7 were loaded at Port Clarence in October 1981 and arrived on site by the end of the month together with the gates for three 31 m spans adjacent to the north bank. The two gate ends were placed in position on piers 6 and 7 early in November. All was now ready for the gate leaf, which was about to be loaded at Port Clarence and due to sail for the Thames early in November. This was not to be, however, as a dispute arose between the dockers on the Tees and the Dock Authority. The barge was not permitted to sail even though the dispute was nothing to do with the GLC or their contractors. There had to be yet another alteration of plan at site. Navigation had to be switched back to the opening between piers 6 and 7, and the gate arm on pier 7 in the span 'C' between piers 7 and 8 set in position. Finally the gate leaf for the span

Placing the first gate leaf, 14 December 1981 (courtesy of Davy Cleveland Barrier Consortium)

121

between piers 7 and 8, which had rested on its barge in the Royal Docks for nearly a year, was put in position, but even this operation almost had to be cancelled at the last minute. The operation was planned for the morning of 14 December. A blizzard set in during the early hours of the morning with strong winds, but the forecast was optimistic that later that morning better conditions would move in. A courageous decision was taken to go ahead and place the gate leaf. Soon after 7 a.m. the weather improved, the wind dropped and the sun came out. The two heavy-lift cranes from Neptun had lifted the gate leaf in preparation for the operation. The cranes with their 1500 t burden moved majestically into position and the gate leaf was lowered into place on the two gate ends ready for bolting up. By midday the first 61 m gate leaf of the Thames Barrier was in place. Christmas 1981 for those involved with the barrier project was a much happier occasion than had appeared possible even a short time before. At last sheer determination and perseverance had triumphed over the problems, setbacks and mischance that had appeared to dog the project. No doubt John Fletcher, Chairman of the Davy Cleveland Barrier Consortium, Bill Maisey the Project Director and Dick Thorp the Site Manager enjoyed their Christmas dinner a lot more than they might have done.

After the traumatic events of 1981, 1982 seemed almost an anti-climax. The dockers' dispute on the Tees dragged on for some time but was eventually settled. The remaining gates, gate ends and radius arms were loaded up and transported to the Thames, and placed in position. The last gate leaf was bolted up, the machinery installed and connected. Just before low water in the early hours of the morning of Sunday 31 October, all the barrier gates were raised and the first full closure had been achieved—the barrier was operational and if a surge tide arrived the gates could be closed and London saved from a disastrous flood! The first closure had been made at low water for a period of less than three hours. It was still necessary to test the structure by closing the gates with the tide flooding at maximum velocity. This was done on the following Sunday, the gates being closed at half flood just before 2 p.m., and opened at half ebb, 8.28 p.m. During this period the maximum difference of level across the gates built up to 4.0 m. This produced a load of over 2600 t on each of the 61 m gates, and this load was carried with no apparent effect. This was to be expected as it was only a fraction of the full design load, but at the same time it was equivalent to closure against a surge tide with a high surge component. Analysis of the gate deflections showed these to be as predicted. After the first full closures there was still a good deal of work to be done. Temporary electric cables and switchgear had to be replaced with the permanent units, remedial painting of the gates was necessary where the lifting lugs had been welded on, and

Full closure of the Thames Barrier, 7 November 1982 (courtesy of the Greater London Council)

numerous other minor items needed sorting out before the job could be finally declared finished. However, but for the final polishing, the main objective of making the barrier effective had been achieved.

12

Other contracts

The previous chapters have dealt with the major contracts for the construction of the civil engineering works, gates and machinery. There were also a number of other contracts which, although small in value, were vital to the successful completion of the barrier.

Probably the most important were those dealing with the main shafts and bearings about which the gates rotate, and the heavy steel castings which were built into the piers to carry the shafts. The shaft support structures took the form of a large hollow cylinder, in the case of the 61 m gates, 3 m in diameter, with a bolting flange either at one end only or in other cases at both ends, strengthened with circumferential and longitudinal ribs. The structure has four feet to enable it to be positioned accurately in the pier and in the case of the large units for the 61 m gates, weighed 125 t.

Tenders were invited from a number of firms both in the UK and on the Continent for the contract to supply five large structures for the 61 m gates and four smaller units for the 31 m gates. Voest, the Austrian National Steel Corporation, submitted a very competitive price which was accepted after a small group of engineers from the Consulting Engineers and the GLC had inspected the manufacturing facilities at their works at Linz, which were excellent. The contract, for a sum of £729 000, was awarded at the end of March 1974 and manufacture of the patterns for the main castings started in June, with the first casting being poured in August. At this stage the contract had run into financial difficulties as the pound sterling had fallen against the Austrian schilling. Payments under the contract were in sterling, hence the problem. To overcome this difficulty, Voest proposed to subcontract some of the structures to the Belgian firm of Cockerill—Ougrée at Liège, as this would reduce transport costs. Rendel Palmer & Tritton reported favourably on the facilities at Liège and this arrangement was approved. Deliveries went ahead reasonably in step with the other contracts and the last unit was delivered by April 1977. As units for the 61 m gates weighed 125 t, a good deal of thought had to be given to finding a satisfactory route to the site! Due to the delays on contract 3, storage had to be arranged for these structures until the work on the piers was sufficiently advanced for them to be installed. A trial assembly of a shaft support structure and a shaft was carried out at the Sheffield Works of Davy-Loewy to check that there would be no snags when it was necessary to bolt up the shaft as part of the operation of installing the gate arm. Under contract 3, a special rig was supplied by Sparrows to lift these heavy structures out of the barge which brought them to site and to traverse them across the piers to the precise position where they were to be placed. It was vital that these units were positioned very accurately as the shaft position determined the clearance between the gate and the concrete sill. The requirement was that the centre line of the structure was to lie within a 5 mm radius circle. This was achieved in all cases, the maximum error being 3 mm.

The steel shafts which were bolted to the shaft support structures also formed a separate contract. This was awarded to the British Steel Corporation for a sum of £372 400. The shafts were to be cast in $1\%\,Mn-1\%\,Cr-Ni-Mo$ steel with a yield stress of 432 N/mm^2 and an ultimate stress of 586 N/mm^2. The contract ran from 1 May 1974 and was completed by February 1977. It involved the supply of eight shafts for the 61 m gates and four shafts for the 31 m gates. The casting, forging and machining of the shafts was carried out at the River Don Works of the British Steel Corporation and was a very impressive operation. The shaft for the 61 m gate started off as a 180 t billet which, after preliminary forging, was heated to a good red heat in a gas-fired furnace, and then placed in a 12 000 t press where it was squeezed into a die to form it to the correct shape. After this process it was removed to the annealing pit and machined to the required dimensions, finishing up as a shaft weighing 48 t. There was an initial setback to this contract when a fire at one of BSC's works destroyed two electric furnaces and put the work back several weeks. However, this delay did not affect the critical path for the gate contract, and all the shafts were duly handed over.

The third of this group of contracts was for the bearings which are fitted on the shafts and about which the gates rotate. At an early stage in the design of the machinery for operating the gates, an appraisal of all the types of bearing which could meet the required duty was carried out. Consideration was given to the use of spherical roller bearings, hydrostatic bearings, or spherical plain bearings using a dry lubricant. The last of these was chosen as the most reliable. A fractured roller in a

Forging a main shaft (courtesy of Sheffield Forgemasters Ltd)

roller bearing would cause very serious problems, and the oil supply could fail with the hydrostatic bearing. The decision to bolt the shaft to the shaft support structure concreted in the pier was taken, since fitting the bearing in the pier and fixing the shaft to the gate arm would impose a large bending moment on the gate arm when the full load was applied to the gate.

The dynamic load on the 61 m gate trunnion bearing is 2600 t, and the static load due to the weight of the gate and the hydraulic loading is over 5000 t. Once the decision had been taken to use these bearings, the same

Machining a main shaft (courtesy of Sheffield Forgemasters Ltd)

type of bearing was specified for the radius arms, connecting rods and links. It was also decided to use linear bearings of this type for the crosshead guides. In all, 142 rotational bearings and 256 linear bearings were required. Tender documents were issued for the manufacture of these bearings. A favourable tender was received from Merriman Inc. of Boston, Massachusetts, for bearings of their lubrite design. These bearings are of the spherical type, the inner ball being of a Ni—Al corrosion-resisting bronze, with trepanned holes all over the spherical surface into which a solid dry lubricant is injected. The whole surface in addition is coated with a thick layer of the lubricant. The outer race is of corrosion-resistant stainless steel which is centrifugally cast. In addition, as a secondary means of lubrication and to protect the shaft and housing against corrosion, the whole assembly is packed with grease. The largest of these bearings, for the 61 m gates, has an outside diameter of 1500 mm and a width of 620 mm, and weighs 13 t. The linear bearings for the crosshead guides consist of stainless steel backing plates to which woven Teflon is bonded as a dry lubricant. The guide surfaces are of aluminium bronze to prevent corrosion and the crossheads are fitted with wipers to remove dust and grit as the crosshead moves along the guide.

The contract, value £1.33 million, was placed with Merriman in July 1974, and was completed by April 1977. The casting of the inner and outer races was carried out at the Wisconsin Centrifugal Works at Waukesha, north of Chicago. The trepanning, coating with the special

Lubrite bearing for 61 m gate (courtesy of Merriman Inc.)

solid lubricant and the assembly of the bearings took place at the Merriman Works at Boston. These were some of the largest bearings that the firm had ever produced.

A separate contract was let to Sindall Construction Ltd of Cambridge for an important group of buildings, including on the south bank the control building, generator house, workshop, substations, car park, services subways, operating deck and ramps, public walkway, gatehouse and boundary walls. On the north bank, substations, service subways, gatehouse and boundary walls were required. The most impressive of the group is the control building, which is on the centre line of the barrier and rises 60 m above ground level, giving a good view over to the north bank and also upriver and downriver. This building is the nerve centre of the barrier with the main control panel, generator control panel, tide gauges and telecommunications equipment. The generator house contains three 1½ MW diesel generator sets, any one of which is capable of operating the barrier under emergency conditions. Most of these buildings are supported on piles and have frames either of reinforced concrete or steel. All the major buildings have stainless steel roofs to harmonise with the pier roofs.

This was a large and important contract worth £5.5 million. Work on

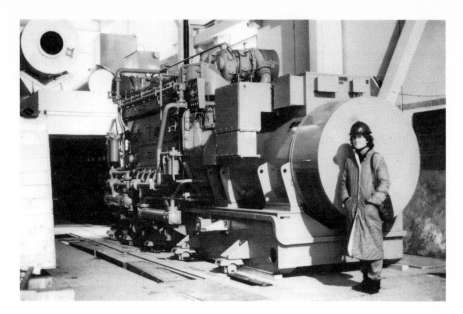

1.5 MW diesel generator

the contract started in October 1977 and went ahead steadily, which was remarkable in view of the complex operations going on all around. There were sundry alarms and excitements but generally the various difficulties were overcome satisfactorily. Another group of contracts covered the diesel generators, the high-voltage switchgear and transformers, main control panels and equipment, local control panels, low-voltage switchgear, services, lifts, and navigation lights. The generators were supplied by Mirrlees Blackstone Ltd, the high-voltage switchgear and transformers by GEC Distribution Switchgear Ltd, the control panels and equipment by Henry Williams Ltd, the services by Balfour Kilpatrick Ltd, local control panels by British Brown Boveri Ltd, the low voltage switchgear by Sunderland Forge and Engineering Ltd, lifts by Evans Lifts Ltd of Leicester and navigation lights by Aga (UK) Ltd. A further contract was let for the south bank ancillary works to John Mowlem and Co. Ltd. The letting of these separate contracts, particularly the two with foreign firms, put a considerable administrative load on the GLC staff as the client authority. Cyril Hart, the Branch Administrative Officer, and his staff did a sterling job in getting all these contracts finalised without any undue delay.

13

Flood defences downstream

The Thames Flood Prevention Investigation had been undertaken because of the flood threat to London, but it soon became obvious that this would involve flood protection to the whole of the Thames Estuary, since it would be illogical, and politically very emotive, to protect areas of Bermondsey and Bow to a higher standard than Erith and Tilbury. A variation of standard could be justified, however, on a cost—benefit basis as this would be in accord with the national policy. As a result the 1000-year return period high water, which has approximately a 1 in 1000 chance in a year with an allowance for the estimated adverse trend of high waters compared with land levels, plus an increment to allow for any adverse effect of barrier operation, was adopted as the standard for the whole estuary, from the barrier to Southend's eastern boundary on the north bank, and the Cliffe Marshes on the south bank, for urban areas where a cost—benefit analysis showed that this could be justified. A conference was held by MAFF in 1971 where a profile of flood levels was agreed. This became known as the Medway standard.

The length of banks which had to be strengthened was over 70 miles, and the cost was about £300 million. In addition to the bank work, five minor barriers were constructed and two very substantial flood gates provided for the main entrances of the Royal and Tilbury Docks. Three of the 'minor' barriers are large structures in their own right, the Barking Creek, Dartford Creek and Fobbing Horse barriers, with main openings of 38 m, 30 m and 36 m respectively. The dock entrance gates are also large structures with gates 33.5 m and 30.5 m wide and over 17 m deep. The gates weigh over 200 t. These dock storm gates are larger than the gate of the tidal barrier protecting Kingston upon Hull from storm surges from the Humber estuary, which has a gate of 30 m span, 10.6 m deep, weighing 200 t.

Although the same 1000-year return period surge tide standard was applied throughout the whole of the Thames Estuary, the actual level of the flood defences varied for two reasons. As explained in Chapter 2, normal tides rise to higher levels as they move up the estuary towards the tidal limit. A normal spring tide will reach a level 1 m higher at London Bridge than it attained at Southend. The other factor is the expected wave height. This depends on the degree of exposure of the site and the available 'fetch' for the gale force winds which generate the waves. The profile agreed at the Medway Conference by MAFF in 1971 was a 'still water' profile, and additional height had to be added for wave action. In the case of earth banks, the crest may dry out and an allowance has to be made for this effect. In the GLC area, which was comparatively sheltered, masonry or concrete walls had an additional 0.3 m added as 'freeboard', earth banks had an additional 0.9 m. In the outer estuary, earth banks were raised above the Medway profile by as much as 1.3 m.

The Medway profile had included an allowance for the effect of operation of the barrier. This varied from 0.2 m at the barrier site to 0.1 m at Southend. In the early years a good deal of importance was attached to the need to complete the bank work before the barrier was finished. The idea seemed to have taken root that as the GLC were investigating ways of protecting the estuary against surge tides, these were caused by the GLC. The obvious fact that surge tides would occur, irrespective of what the GLC did, seemed to have little significance. In fact the reverse was true; the bank-raising work carried out in the downriver areas in 1954 and 1955 increased the risk to London by preventing overspill on to the marshlands.

The technical problems encountered in the construction of the banks downriver and of the smaller barriers were as difficult as, and in some cases more difficult than, those of the main barrier. Tidal estuaries are renowned for difficult foundation conditions and the Thames is no exception. Under surge tide conditions, uplift can occur when the peats and muds of the estuary are underlain by pervious gravels and sands. In many cases access for heavy plant was difficult. The biggest problem was not an engineering one, however. This was the problem of negotiating with a large number of owners and occupiers details of their requirements affecting the design of the flood defences, and terms and conditions of entry for the purpose of carrying out the construction work. In the GLC area of responsibility alone, some 70 different firms, authorities or individuals were involved. Since each property had to be given individual treatment, only a limited degree of standardisation of design could be used. The difficulties of carrying out the work without drastically disrupting the business activities taking place were also considerable, and inevitably some degree of compromise had to be achieved. In very few cases could the whole of a particular frontage be occupied at one time and the civil engineering contractor be given a free run to organise his work in the most efficient manner.

These bank contracts had one supreme and overriding advantage, however: it was possible to divide the whole length into sections which resulted in contracts of from £2—6 million in value and of about two years' duration. Under the conditions of recession in civil engineering construction, this value and duration of contract made them very attractive to contracting firms. The contracts were not so large as to endanger the financial position of the firm if it went 'sour' and the duration not so long as to tie up valuable resources of skilled manpower and plant should the market position improve.

The conditions imposed by the PLA for the gates for closing the main locks of the Royal and Tilbury groups of docks were onerous, although not unreasonable from the PLA's point of view. An unobstructed area was required along the whole length of the lock to permit free access for ship handling. Add to this the requirement of getting the gate weighing several hundred tons in position in about one hour from the order to close, and the magnitude of the problem becomes apparent. A solution simple in principle, but alas not quite so easy to put into practice, was devised. This consisted of a carriage that was able to move on rollers, carrying the gate in the horizontal position. The carriage and gate normally are parked well clear of the sides of the lock, but when necessary can be run forward along ways at right angles to the axis of the lock. The gate launching carriage carries the gate at the rear end which enables the nose of the carriage to traverse the lock and to land on rollers on the far bank, before the centre of gravity of the structure has passed the last point of support on the home bank. The carriage continues to traverse across the lock until the gate is in position where it can be swung down under the control of winches until it closes the waterway of the lock. The surge tide will then be prevented from passing through the lock to flood the dock system and the surrounding areas.

Drop gates were provided for the 'mini' barriers at Barking and Dartford Creeks. In the case of Barking, a single gate is used, but the Dartford Creek Barrier has identical and interchangeable gates, each capable of closing off half the depth of the waterway and being used one above the other to shut off the whole opening. In the case of malfunctioning of either gate, the remaining gate could be lowered to close the lower part of the waterway. This would check the inflowing water until about two hours before high water. From then on the gate would be overtopped, but due to the reduced area the flow would be restricted and the scale of flooding much reduced.

Design conditions varied widely for the flood defences for the various frontages downriver of the main barrier. Most of the work in the GLC area consisted of steel sheet piles driven into Thames Ballast or the Chalk, with a concrete capping wall or relieving platform. Where necessary, thrust and overturning moments are resisted by steel 'H' piles. In other areas, the flood defences have been provided economically by earth banks.

In the GLC area of responsibility there were 14.5 miles of banks out of a total downriver figure of 70 miles. The GLC area included three miles on the north bank, from the barrier to Barking Creek, and 11.5 miles on the south bank. Two miles of the southern banks were along Dartford Creek, and protection here was provided by the Dartford Creek Barrier, designed by Sir Bruce White, Wolfe Barry and Partners, with Southern Water Authority as the Clients. The GLC contributed 25% of the cost of this barrier on account of the protection afforded to banks in the GLC area. The GLC bank work therefore covered 12.5 miles and was divided into 20 contracts, valued at about £65 million.

During the feasibility stage, downriver bank work was the responsibility of John Holloway in the investigation team. After the passing of the Barrier Act a design team was set up headed by Henry Colley who had been the Agent for John Mowlem on the reconstruction of London Bridge. He subsequently moved on to the Architect's Department, and Cecil Brown became responsible for bank design. When construction got under way, a contract co-ordinating team was set up, headed by Harold Bubbers who had considerable contracting experience with Sir Robert McAlpine.

As already mentioned, negotiations with frontagers on the detail design of their flood defences proved time consuming. Delay on the main barrier was not unwelcome in this respect, as completion of downriver flood defences in step with the date when the barrier was operable had become a political issue. Activity inevitably expands to fill the time available, and there was a considerable group of contracts let in the last two-and-a-half years before the barrier was operable. This produced a peak administrative load, but all contracts were let and completed on time as a result of a magnificent combined effort by engineers and administrators alike. A schedule of downriver contracts is included in Appendix 5.

14

Barrier operation

The effectiveness of a barrier as a tidal flood defence structure depends entirely on closure of the gates in sufficient time to prevent water levels upstream exceeding the top of the flood defences. The reader will rightly comment that this is obvious, but it is remarkable how easily otherwise sensible people lose sight of this basic fact. It is essential to examine this operation from first principles and to assess very realistically the reliability of each and every link in the chain of decision. The basic elements of the operation are: decision to close the barrier in adequate time, and effective means of translating that decision into the physical closure of all the gates. The decision to close is dependent on adequate data being available on the levels which the incoming tide will reach. Reliable information is available on the normal astronomical tides, but these are subject to modification due to meteorological conditions. The estimation of the 'surge component' is not so simple.

As already described, serious research into this problem started after the high surge tide of 1928 when 14 people were drowned in London. Doodson of the Liverpool Tidal Institute, working in collaboration with Dines of the Meteorological Office, showed that on those occasions when high waters in the Thames Estuary were more than 4 ft above the astronomically predicted value, this was far more often associated with strong north-westerly winds than with easterly winds, which might be considered more likely to cause high waters. On the basis of this work a rudimentary warning system was established, the Meteorological Office passing a warning to Scotland Yard if northerly or north-westerly gales were expected to occur at a time of the twice-monthly spring tides. After the floods of 1953, a full warning service was established under the administration of the Ministry of Agriculture, Fisheries and Food, housed at the Meteorological Office (now at Bracknell), with a staff of four officers of the Hydrographic Department of the Royal Navy to operate it. Initially the method used to estimate the surge component was that suggested by Corkan of the Liverpool Tidal Institute who proposed an equation based on the 'residual' (the difference between the astronomically predicted tide and the actual tide) at Dunbar modified by meteorological data on wind velocities and directions at Fair Isle and in the North Sea, to forecast the surge residual at Southend. A set of equations was subsequently developed which enabled the high water residual at Wick to be used to estimate the residual at Tyne, and so down the coast to Southend. This method has generally worked effectively, but due to the empirical nature of the system it is subject to errors in practice. Mean errors are about 0.2—0.3 m, with a few errors of 0.6 m and very occasionally as much as 1 m. The method permits an update of the surge estimate as results come in from tide gauges down the east coast. The high tide at Immingham occurs six hours before that at Southend, and this provides a very useful update on the way the surge is developing or fading.

Since the empirical system has these known shortcomings, a system of forecasting has been developed making use of the Meteorological Office atmospheric model, linked to the IOS mathematical model and capable of calculating water movements in the sea. Initially the sea model did not include astronomical tide movements, but subsequently was developed to include tides as well. This was an important step, since tide—surge interaction is an important factor in the movement and magnitude of the surge in shallow waters. The results obtained so far have been encouraging and as experience is gained there is no doubt that the system will be developed and refined to be a very effective tool.

The situation over the system for estimating the magnitude of the surge component of any tide is therefore reasonably satisfactory. There is on the one hand the tried and tested empirical method, with known shortcomings which are allowed for by adding to any surge forecast an agreed increment of height, actually 0.3 m. On the other hand there is the promising 'new boy' in the guise of the interlinked mathematical models of atmosphere and tide which is fully expected to be the front runner in the years to come.

We now move on to the next state—translation of the estimate of the surge component on the incoming tide into a decision to close the barrier. For each day of the year there will be a 'danger level' at Southend based on the upland flow of the Thames and the forecast wind velocities in the estuary. High upland flow can raise levels by nearly 1 m in the Richmond area, but only 0.1 m at Woolwich. Strong easterly or westerly winds in the estuary will cause differences of 0.3 m at London Bridge. From this level will be deduced the 0.3 m 'margin of error' referred to above. Should the surge component estimated at any stage as the high water moves down the coast from Wick in the north of Scotland, when added to the level predicted for the astronomic tide, exceed the danger level less the 0.3 m then stand-by action will be taken to close the barrier, the final decision being taken about six hours before high water at the barrier site. There will always be a number of occasions when, after the event, it will be apparent that the barrier was closed unnecessarily. No matter; better to close 100 times when not necessary, than to fail to close once when it was necessary. Transmission of data from Bracknell to the barrier site will be by both radio and land line to guard against any communications failure. In addition, computer resources will be available at the barrier site using a modified version of the IOS numerical model of the southern North Sea to process the data received from the Meteorological Office, together with tide gauge data from as far afield as Immingham to give the Barrier Controller his own independent assessment of the surge situation. The computer program will inform the Controller of the optimum time of closure and the best closure technique to be adopted to eliminate any adverse effect downriver.

When the decision has been taken to close the barrier on the meteorological and tidal information received, what action is then initiated? On receipt of the 'alert' from the Storm Tide Warning Service up to twelve hours before the likely time of overtopping of banks in Central London, or on receipt of news of dangerously high water levels on the north-east coast together with high wind velocities in the North Sea, the duty officers at the barrier site will have been reinforced by the operating team headed by the Duty Barrier Controller. Power supplies from the national grid on north and south banks will have been checked. The on-site generators will have been run up and the hydraulic power packs run to check pressure and availability. Preliminary action will have been taken to disengage gate locks and bring all the machinery to a full state of readiness. As soon as it is apparent that a barrier closure is likely, a preliminary warning will be given to all shipping likely to pass through the barrier site. A warning of closure to all shipping will be issued, normally two hours before closure of the gates, except under conditions of some exceptional emergency when this period may have to be reduced. When the warning period has expired, gate closure will start with the falling radial gates close to the north and south banks, then the main gates are closed, the two centre gates being the last to close. The whole operation will take only half an hour. The gates will remain fully closed for the optimum period while the incoming tide surges up against them. After the tide has been checked for about an hour, the gates can be raised so that the lower edge of the gate is clear of the sill in the river bed by about 1 m. This will allow sufficient water to pass under the gate to

136

Gate in undershot flow position closed

give water levels upriver equal to those of a normal spring tide. The 'drawdown effect' on water levels downriver of the barrier produced by this mode of operation will ensure that the high-water levels downriver do not exceed those which would have been reached if the barrier had not been closed. Once the main gates are closed a differential in water levels will build up across the structure. After high water, as the tide downriver ebbs away, this difference of level will reduce and once the level upriver is within about 0.2 m of that downriver the main gates may be opened again and the river flow restored to normal. Experience may allow this difference of level to be increased, but too large a differential when the gates are opened could cause excessive velocities in the river and might cause scour of the river bed. It is unlikely that this would be serious, but at the same time there is little to be gained by rushing the operation to save a few minutes. Increased flow under the gates would be a better method of reducing the closure period if this is necessary. It is expected that the average full closure will last about five hours.

To provide the necessary operating team, key personnel will be on site on a shift system so that a full operating team can be at their posts within an hour under any conditions.

On the basis of probabilities, two or three closures per year to hold back dangerous surge tides will be necessary over the next decade, but as sea levels rise ever higher compared with the land levels, closures will become more frequent and in the 21st century up to ten closures a year may be quite normal. In view of this, anxiety has been expressed on the effective life of the barrier. The design was of course based on the surge tide expected on a 1 in 1000 chance in a year, combined with an allowance of adverse change of water levels of 0.8 m per century, or 8 mm per year to the year 2030. The design of the gates allows for a very large difference to be built up across them, since in the early days the potential of undershot flow below the gates was not fully realised, and it was considered desirable to have gates which could be closed at any stage of the tide without any fear that they might become overloaded and strained. As a result, when in the fully closed position, the gates can accept a very considerable depth of flow over the top edge without any ill effects. The upriver section of the Thames forms a very large reservoir, some 26 miles long and about 4 square miles in area. If the gates were overtopped by 0.8 m in the year 2130 by the then 1 in 1000 year tide, the pond upriver would rise by only about 1 ft!

Are the gates therefore excessively strong? This brings in another operational hazard, that of ship collision. It is always possible that a ship could get out of control when passing the barrier and strike the structure a glancing blow with either bow or stern. The gates and gate arms are built of heavy steel plate, 40 mm and 50 mm thick and the structure is designed to deflect or 'spring' under load. We therefore have a strong and resilient structure being hit by a vessel which is an eggshell in comparison. Some damage might occur to the operating machinery, but it is difficult to visualise how serious damage could be done to the gates. Damage to the main machinery is allowed for by the disconnection arrangement in the main link from the radius arm to the gate end. A damaged shift and latch mechanism could be lifted clear of the gate end. The gates can be closed quite effectively by operation of the machinery from one end only. In the very unlikely event of a ship being sunk in one of the main openings, closure of the other gates would cause a high-velocity flow through the obstructed opening which would probably move the obstructing vessel clear of the gate and allow it to be closed. This might be a rather exciting operation but it would certainly be effective! Should a ship get stuck in the opening it would restrict flow through the structure to an extent which would still enable the barrier to be effective.

15

The future (RWH)

The previous chapters have described the long haul from the traumatic floods of 1953 to the present day when the Thames Barrier is capable of being operated to hold back a high surge tide from flooding into Central London—thirty years of discussion, argument, decision, planning, design, construction and operation. Why did it take so long, could corners have been cut and the necessary protection have been achieved in less time? It is worth thinking about these things; fate has been kind to us, but it might easily have been otherwise. One has only to remember Hamburg in 1962.

Of the earlier schemes, in the authors' opinion the best was the drop-gate barrier proposed for the centre of Long Reach. Should the PLA's objections on the grounds of the navigational risks have been overruled and, if so, why was this not done? At that time there were many claims on the available resources for building and civil engineering works—housing, motorways, and the polluted state of the Thames right through the heart of the capital city. One suspects that it was not too unwelcome to be able to put the problem of tidal flooding of London into the 'too difficult' pigeonhole. So the M1 motorway was built rather than the Thames Barrier. Nearly 25 years after, and without a major flood, it is difficult to say the wrong decision was taken. How about the clean-up of the Thames, costing many millions of pounds and gaining world-wide recognition as a major victory in the struggle to reduce pollution of the environment in a major city? Should this have been delayed while the Thames flood protection works went ahead? One of the authors cannot find it in his heart to condemn that decision! However, it might well have been a better course to have cut down on housing, the building of high-rise blocks of flats, for example, and to have got on with the flood works. Housing at the time was a very politically sensitive issue, and one suspects that any cutback on housing would have produced unfavourable political reactions.

Once the decision was taken to look upriver from Long Reach, it is difficult to see why so much time was wasted investigating schemes for Crayfordness which, apart from having good foundation conditions, was a most unsuitable site. This was the site chosen by the PLA, and one suspects that it was for this reason that time and effort had to be expended in examining ways in which an effective barrier could be constructed on this site. Any body promoting such a project would not have a good image with the Parliamentary Committee investigating the proposal if they had not examined schemes for the site recommended by the statutory navigation authority! When the schemes were produced and evaluated, there was a further delay until Professor Bondi's report gave the common-sense recommendation of looking for a more suitable site further upriver.

The GLC investigation led to the choice of the Woolwich site and the design with four main openings of 61 m. In view of the subsequent closure of the West India Docks, was this design too generous in the provisions and could a more economic design have been put forward with fewer and smaller openings? Experience during the later stages of construction showed that the needs of navigation could be met by one 61 m opening in operation. Most of the construction problems were with the building of the piers of the structure, and therefore it would appear illogical to select a design which had more piers than the structure actually built. By making the spans all 50 m, but with gates of varying depth, the number of piers could be reduced by one; navigation spans could be reduced to three, to allow for maintenance on one of the main gates. Overall cost of the structure might have been reduced by 12—15%; a useful economy but not of great magnitude. The decision to use the rising sector gate seemed sound at the time, but would the use of drop gates have been more sensible? The cost of gate, counterweights and operating machinery would have been much the same, but the smaller sills would have led to further economy with the civil engineering work. Provision of two separate access subways, necessary for the duplicated power and control network, would limit the scope for economy, however. A further saving of 5% might be achieved. So a structure might be designed for present navigation conditions some 15—20% cheaper than the structure actually built. Drop gates of course have the advantage that they can be closed without any external power by lowering the gate under control of brakes. Closing all ten gates of the Thames Barrier without any electric control gear would be quite an undertaking! Drop gates have their maintenance problems, whether the gates are suspended on steel cables or chains. The robust machinery, and the simple manner in which the rising sector gates rotate about their pivots, inspires confidence compared with lowering a very heavy gate 50 m down to the bed of the fast-flowing tidal river, taking care that it does not get out of level and jam in its guides.

This book would not be complete without some comments on the cost of the project. The system adopted by the GLC has been to estimate on current prices at the time of the estimate and not to guess at a possible decline in the purchasing power of the pound sterling in the future. On this basis everyone knows what they are doing, and crystal ball gazing on what is going to happen to the purchasing power of the pound in the years to come is avoided. It may be argued that wrong decisions may be taken on the allocation of resources on this basis. When the purchasing power of the pound falls, it does not mean that more real resources, tons of steel, tons of concrete or man-hours are used up, but that more pounds are needed to buy those resources. The costs of the barrier escalated, but the quantities of steel and concrete used are very close to the quantities included in the original tenders. The man-hours were considerably higher due to low productivity (see below).

Early estimates by the Consulting Engineers had to be revised due to inflation and other factors. On the receipt of the tenders for the main contracts, a reasonably sound basis for an estimate had been achieved. All the major contracts were index linked and therefore subject to variation if the indices of costs of labour, plant and basic materials varied, either up or down, although indices go up much more often than they go down. On this basis the cost of the barrier at October 1973 price levels was £110.7 million. The contract 3 (the civil engineering contract) tender was heavily qualified and therefore did not claim to represent the whole cost of the civil engineering works. In later years, interviewers from the media were wont to ask why tenders were not called on a fixed-price basis. On being told that no reputable contractor in his right mind would submit a tender for a large long-term contract on that basis, they were left speechless, but obviously of the mind that there should be a law to make fixed-price tendering compulsory. One doubts that they themselves would sign a contract for a fixed salary for five or six years ahead except on the most generous terms.

The completion cost of the barrier was about £440 million. Of the increase of £329.3 million, it can be calculated from the price index figures used that about 70% of this increase has been due to inflation. Of the remaining increased cost, about 5% has been due to refinement of design which included such items as additional reinforcement in the sills between the piers to allow for possible uplift due to water pressure on the underside during certain conditions of closure of the barrier when in operation. Other items in this category were stairs instead of ladders in

141

the piers to meet requirements of the Health and Safety at Work Act, small increases in the foundation depths of the piers and similar items. Of the remaining sum, about 10% can be attributed to construction difficulties not covered in the original tenders, or allowed for in the contingencies such as the uplift problem of pier 7 and the underground obstructions met in driving the piles for the other cofferdams. There remains about 15% which can be allocated to low productivity. This covers the whole range from too optimistic output figures included in the original tender, to overt and covert industrial action, and management shortcomings in the organisation of the work, which includes the very constricted working conditions provided in the design of the cofferdams for the southern piers, and the learning curve in devising the most effective methods of excavating and cleaning up the bottom of the pier cofferdams. It is very difficult to separate these two elements with any degree of accuracy, so it is largely a matter of opinion as to the proportion of cost borne by one element or the other.

Are there any lessons to be learnt from the experience of carrying out this project? With a large contract, it is certainly desirable to conclude a binding site agreement defining conditions of employment and bonus earnings before work starts on site. Where 24-hour working is necessary, the three 8-hour shifts' system has much to commend it compared with working two 12-hour shifts. Firm leadership by a management team who get out of the office and see for themselves what is happening at the work site, and gain the confidence of their workforce that complaints and niggles will be speedily and effectively dealt with, is another essential ingredient for a successful contract. In all this the need for sound planning and careful attention to detail, with sufficient back-up plant to prevent a breakdown or accident halting a vital operation, must not be overlooked. Modern 'management techniques' do not provide a magic wand that will eliminate the need for realistic planning and sheer hard work to get the job running right. These things sound very simple when written down, but alas are much more difficult to put into practice. In the case of the barrier some of these lessons were relearnt the hard way, but success was achieved in the end.

Having looked at past events, perhaps a look to the future would be appropriate? The barrier is now operable as a flood defence structure and will probably be closed two or three times a year in the 1980s, but this is expected to increase on the basis of the past experience of the rise of high waters. In the early part of the 21st century closures may increase to ten times a year. The more frequent the closures, the more attractive the idea becomes of converting the structure into a full barrage, keeping tides out of the upper estuary. A lock system to allow vessels to pass through would be desirable but not essential. If the water level upriver of the barrier were maintained at about the present half-tide level, the gates would be closed at low water, but could be opened for about two hours at half tide to allow movement of shipping through the barrier. Similar action could be taken at half ebb. This would give a tidal range upriver of about 1.7−2.0 m which would have most of the advantages of a tidal regime without the disadvantages of the present high range and high velocities. Ships could pass through without the delay of locking. Since the average water level upriver would approximate to mean tide level, there should be no change in ground-water levels, which was one of the more serious drawbacks of the full barrage schemes. Since times of opening and closing the structure, based on predicted tide times, would be published well in advance, shipping movements could be planned to suit these times. There would be other advantages: the salinity of the water upriver would be reduced as a result of the smaller tidal range, and a fresh-water reservoir 26 miles long and 4 square miles in area would be created in the heart of London. The need for new reservoirs in the rural areas of the Thames Valley would disappear. This supply could be drawn from shallow wells into the Thames Ballast which underlies much of the low-lying area of the tidal river from Hammersmith to Woolwich, and could be used for a range of industrial purposes. Another interesting aspect of barrier operation is the 'once off' closure for recreational purposes. Given sufficient warning to river traffic, a closure of the barrier at half tide on the flood would provide a still-water lake in Central London for 6, 12, 18, or 24 hours. This could be very advantageous for staging a regatta, or water spectacle or similar event. Legal powers for such operation were not conferred on the GLC by the Barrier Act, but Parliament could soon remedy this omission.

The effective life of the barrier has been dealt with but what are the limits of the physical life of the elements of the structure? The life of the barrier piers will be that of the Portland cement used in their construction. Portland cement is considered superior in durability to Roman cement, which is still in good condition at Bath after nearly 2000 years. It would therefore not be unreasonable to suggest a life of 2000 years for the piers. The steel gates, protected by the best paint system that modern technology can devise and backed up by sacrificial anode cathodic protection, should last as well as the wrought iron plates of Brunel's SS Great Britain, and that ship is at Bristol for all to see after 140 years—so let us say the gates will have a life of 200 years. What of the hydraulic machinery, the massive steel cylinders, pistons and connecting rods? The Boulton and Watt beam engine of the Crofton pumping station on the Kennet and Avon Canal, built in 1812, still works satisfactorily after 170 years and there is no reason to suppose that the barrier machinery will not last even longer, indeed it should!

16

Conclusions (SKG)

A catastrophe! An emergency! The government should *do* something about it. Worse, the government should *have done* something about it. The government should be all foreseeing, all wise, all provident. Alas it cannot be. These qualities belong to a higher sphere. There was a catastrophe in 1953. The Thames Barrier was first operated in 1982. If you have read so far without skipping too much, you will know what went on in the intervening period. Contrary to the idea of government having the powers and responsibilities of a father, it does not have infinite powers. It can only act within the law, implementing Acts of Parliament. It is true that in an emergency much more can be done, which can later be covered by retrospective legislation, the government can prepare for emergencies in general. A Civil Contingencies Unit has been set up; local government must now have officers to prepare emergency plans.

Prevention of flooding, and helping those flooded, is normally a matter for the local authority, but of course if the flooding is extensive, help in putting things right may come from many quarters, including the government. In London, in 1953, the areas which could be flooded by a surge tide ran across many local government boundaries; as a result central government took over the task of organising flood precautions, acting as a co-ordinator, or agent, of the local authorities. Hence their representation on the 1928 Committee, the Waverley Committee and the subsequent Thames Technical Panel. The Waverley Committee, driven by its powerful chairman, reported promptly. Nine tenths of its recommendations concerned the east coast and these are not criticised; but its recommendation about London showed a complete failure to grasp the problem. Fortunately this recommendation, which was that the 1953 floods were the worst that should be prepared against in London, was immediately and instinctively rejected by the engineers on the Thames Technical Panel at their first meeting.

The Technical Panel also reported promptly, so where were the rest of those 30 years lost? Some of them were not lost but went into the designing and building of the barrier; no time was lost here in excess of the normal delays on large civil engineering constructions, especially those of a novel character. There was less 'overrun' with the barrier than with some other projects of the same complexity and size, such as atomic power stations.

The action by the PLA in going back on their agreement to a site for the barrier in Long Reach caused the loss of three years spent on investigations and designs for that site. Moreover, their subsequent insistence on the Crayfordness site, with a requirement for a 1400 ft opening, caused the loss of three more years for work on new designs. But here the PLA are not alone in being open to criticism. As Professor Bondi emphasised, the proponents of the barrier should have fought the PLA and looked for other sites themselves.

When considering the delays we should perhaps try to put ourselves in the general frame of mind of the times. In 1953 money was very short. Rationing had been more stringent after the Second World War than during it. Financially, Britain was just beginning to recover from the deep depression caused by the war. Everyone looked at large-scale and expensive projects with these matters in mind. There was a vast balance of payments problem. Britain was heavily in debt to the USA. Exports were essential. Britain's greatest port, still the world's greatest port, was vital to the nation's economy. To damage it would be suicidal. The requirements of the Port of London Authority were sacred. Save London from flooding by all means, but do not put the nation's vital exports at risk. So when the PLA suggested (ordained almost) that the barrier should be in the middle of Long Reach, and when this was found to be a possible site on engineering grounds, and indeed a natural one, to stop flooding as high land came down near the river on both banks, the suggestion was naturally adopted. Designs were made for a simple, drop-gate sluice-type barrier for the centre of Long Reach; these satisfied everyone, except the PLA who had, inadvertently or otherwise, now made this site impossible. But still the PLA could not be questioned. Their word was paramount and when they said 'Go to Crayfordness at the head of Long Reach', off went the engineers. It is true that there was a bend there, and that the PLA demanded a navigational opening twice as wide as the length of the longest ships which passed, and the decision to design a barrier at that site did not go through without argument. However, the consulting engineers said that they could devise a barrier to close the immense gap. They prepared designs, but the degree of innovation, although all of it was most ingenious, frightened those who examined the proposal, while the high estimated costs did not encourage an immediate order to proceed.

In engineering terms, it was now back to the drawing board. The previous occasion on which this had happened, when the specification changed from a 500 ft navigable opening to a 1400 ft one, had not produced an encouraging outcome. So it was decided to steep the project in a think tank, in the hope that it would emerge with a more amenable consistency. It did, and, thanks to the compelling arguments of Professor Bondi, the project was started from an excellent position when the drawing board was brought back into use again.

Professor Bondi helped the proponents of the barrier across a notable obstacle. An application for Treasury sanction for a very large sum would have been met with a request for a cost—benefit analysis. As the risk element could only be assessed from very imperfectly understood phenomena, there would have been difficulties. But although it would be very difficult to make a case out on those grounds, it seemed clear from the increasing surge tide levels that something ought to be done. The resolution was fortunate, and in many ways typically English. An eminent mathematician bypassed the morass of statistics, categorised the question as philosophical, and gave the ardently desired practical answer: do it. To ordinary engineers who had long believed that philosophy was mainly the use of meticulous argument from premises carefully chosen to lead to the intended conclusion, this use of the word 'philosophical' was extremely welcome. It solved the deadlock and set everything in motion.

In some ways it was fortunate that the final design of the barrier was delayed until it could have the benefit of the extraordinary blossoming of new ideas in the construction industry to meet the needs of the North Sea oil rigs. These induced an outburst of engineering innovation only to be matched in the world of electronics and in the marvels which enabled man not only to reach the moon but also to return.

In the end the invention of the container, and the consequent decline of London Docks, reduced the width of the navigable opening demanded by the PLA from 500 ft to 200 ft, while the ingenuity of the Consulting Engineers devised the rising sector gate which would span that width. They should also have the credit for their bold return to massive operating machinery which, although reminiscent of ancient beam engines, is entirely suited to its purpose.

On the administrative side, the national and local government machinery worked very slowly. The barrier was only just completed in time. However, for all its slow progress, it was never diverted into the Circumlocution Office. London survived without further incursions by

Neptune, although saved by the skin of its teeth—that skin being the temporary bank raising.

In the Netherlands the battle against Neptune has been long and he has been pushed back to a position where he is very dangerous. The Dutch have a competent government agency, the Rijkswaterstaat, to fight this battle. It is being fought with great success; indeed technically the Dutch are so successful that a recent extension of the flood defences in the Eastern Scheldt seems designed to conserve a river estuary rather than protect land, and this at vast expense.

The problem in Venice is different. The city has been developed in a way that gives every convenience to incoming flood water. Having been built on estuarial mud, it has sunk slowly for natural reasons. Man has accelerated the process in the 20th century by drilling boreholes and pumping water from them. This has now been stopped, but not before shallow flooding of the streets has become frequent. Many schemes to prevent this have been discussed; the favourite is to use inflatable dams across the openings through the Lido, the bank which separates the lagoon containing Venice from the open sea. (The tides which flood Venice are raised by strong winds blowing up the Adriatic Sea.)

Leningrad, like Venice, stands at the end of a long and fairly narrow sea; like Venice it is intersected by canals. From time to time strong winds blowing up the Baltic raise the level of the sea and flood the streets. A great river, the Neva, flows through the city and is bordered by extensive port installations, which complicate the problem. A scheme for a vast dyke enclosing a considerable area of sea off the river mouth, and provided with locks and navigation openings, was just starting when there were objections from Sweden and Finland. Modifications have been discussed, and, in 1983, the scheme is about to be started again.

Hamburg, as already mentioned, was flooded by a 4 m surge in 1962. The problem there was comparatively simple and has been solved by raising the flood banks. The extensive downriver bank raising may well lead to higher flood levels upriver. In the centre of the city, instead of a high and unsightly flood wall, an elevated promenade has been built. Large areas of the port and shipyards are, however, still open to a similar flood; the construction of a barrier, which is understood to have been delayed because of a lack of funds, is still being considered.

So, as slowly as the Thames Barrier project moved, it did no worse than similar ones elsewhere. What lessons are there for the future? Perhaps it would have been better had such a massive project been in the hands of some powerful authority, rather than passing through a series of ad hoc committees? An All Party Select Committee of the House of Commons considered this matter but failed to find any solution. The difference between the way the Thames Technical Panel could advance and the way the GLC got rapidly to grips with the problem is very clear. This lesson should be borne in mind for future projects such as the Severn tidal power scheme, London's third airport and the Channel Tunnel. It is ardently to be hoped that neither these schemes nor any similar ones will be subjected to a public inquiry dealing with the basic need. The need for such major schemes is clearly a matter of public policy and something for which Parliament has been elected. The correct function for such a public inquiry is to discover and set out any local effects of the scheme which are deleterious and indicate how they might be avoided or ameliorated. To have matters of national concern, such as the use or non-use of nuclear power, kicked about around a parish pump is a strange way to determine what is best for the nation. Such extended inquiries have already led to harmful delays, for instance, in completion of urgently needed motorways. The Thames Barrier project was not required to pass through the jaws of such a monster but this lucky escape was fortuitous. If public inquiries had been as much in fashion in the 1950s as they have since become we might still be waiting to start the barrier.

During the barrier investigation there was much interest in combining a road crossing of the river with whatever structure was projected. At the first site for which plans were made, the centre of Long Reach, the proximity of the Dartford Tunnel made a bridge unnecessary. At the second site, at the head of Long Reach, the very wide opening and the fact that the only type of structure considered was the retractable girder, whose installations would not have formed a suitable basis for a bridge, meant that a bridge would have been impossible here. At sites near the centre of London, bridge schemes would have involved long viaduct approaches in order to gain the necessary height for the passage of shipping, 175 ft; this would have had a detrimental effect on the neighbourhood.

There did, however, seem to be a strong demand for a new bridge. One idea was to incorporate a barrier into the design of a bridge that was already being planned. This design, which had been prepared for the City authorities, was for a bridge a few hundred yards below Tower Bridge to take ten traffic lanes. The two halves of this bridge would have been retracted into vast caverns contained under the approach roads whenever a ship wanted to make a ceremonial visit to the Pool of London above Tower Bridge. The idea of combining the bridge with a barrier was discarded as it was thought that a project which involved approach roads for ten lanes of traffic converging on a bridge site would take too long to fit into the barrier scheme.

At the time of designing the barrier, investigation was made into the possibility of including a bridge in the barrier structure. Fortunately, this was not done. The piers in the river would have been the parts principally affected, and there were sufficient difficulties without adding the support of a bridge to their functions. The site now favoured for a bridge is well downriver of the barrier and clear of the docks.

Much interest was also expressed in the idea of harnessing the potential of the barrier for producing hydroelectric power. The use of Old London Bridge for water wheels to pump water has already been mentioned. Normally hydroelectric power stations are sited on dams across flowing rivers. Sometimes barrages across tidal estuaries can be used; the Rance scheme near St Malo in France is one such scheme and ideas have been put forward for using the estuary of the River Severn.

The Severn Estuary is one of the most favourable sites for the harnessing of tidal energy in the world, having a tidal range of over 40 ft. In the wide spaces of the Severn there are more possibilities for such a development than in the limited space in the Thames. Under examination since 1927, and recently investigated by a committee under the chairmanship of Sir Hermann Bondi, the only recommendation was for further research. The great possibilities of the Severn were unfortunately opposed on account of the very numerous and extensive secondary effects that the scheme would have involved. The French 'Rance' scheme was built as a prestige project, but with the increase in cost of oil has become economic: it is the only significant tidal power scheme in existence.

Generating electricity from the tides is not as simple as it might seem at first sight. Nevertheless, the possibility was kept in mind at all stages of the barrier project until it was clear that the barrier would be open for shipping except when resisting a surge tide, which ruled out the generation of electricity.

The architectural treatment of the piers of the barrier has been generally favourably received. The roofs over the machinery on each pier are made of glittering stainless steel, curved in two dimensions. A similar novelty, used on the roof of the Sydney Opera House, attracted a great deal of criticism. The roof shapes were thought to suggest sails. The Opera House is, however, on the edge of the harbour which does seem to justify the 'sail' idea. The barrier shapes suggest upturned boats, looking for all the world as though Old Peggotty lived there.

The scintillating roofs are very much more apparent to the public than the massive essential parts of the barrier, most of which are below water at normal times. As the architecture of the barrier looms so much larger than the engineering, it is perhaps worthwhile looking at the relations between architects and engineering structures. More often than not, engineers, when designing structures which intrude massively on the environment, have appealed to architects in order to make them acceptable. Tower Bridge is an example of extensive architectural treatment;

the tubular bridge and the suspension bridge across the Menai Strait are less forceful examples. With the fine suspension bridges across the Firth of Forth, the Severn and the Humber, bridges which are intrinsically beautiful, the architect had little to do.

In his normal work, the design of buildings, the architect's task falls into three parts: organisation of space to suit the purpose, design of a sound structure, and 'clothing'. The clothes are the most obvious part: they may be classical, gothic, stockbroker-Tudor or whatever. From the mixed-up Germany of 1919 came Bauhaus—entirely functional, no clothes at all, sheer *Nacht kultur*. Recently the Centre Pompidou in Paris turned the building inside out and draped the entrails over the carcass. Architects have a great repertoire of styles. Success has been achieved with most of them when used skilfully and with a proper regard to the environment.

How should we see the problems of the barrier as it appeared to the architects? The most important factor was that they had a clear field. Out in the middle of the river, with nothing but unobtrusive industrial structures along the bank, they were not called upon to harmonise with anything nor was there anything to clash with.

The barrier was a very important structure which, if nothing were done about it, would make no visual impact. The areas available for architectural treatment, the tops of the piers, were small. How then to emphasise the importance of the structure? Looked at as the answer to this problem, the unusual shapes and glittering surfaces of the roofs are an excellent solution, like a Royal Ball dress with which the Good Fairy architects have adorned what might have been a Cinderella structure. It now takes its place beside Tower Bridge as a symbol of the Thames.

Bibliography

This bibliography not only lists sources used by the authors, but is also intended to act as a guide to readers who require further information on any aspect of London's tidal flood problem and its solution.

ALLEN F.H. *et al.* Model experiments on the storm surge of 1953 in the Thames Estuary and the reduction of future surges. *Proc. Instn Civ. Engrs*, 1955, Part III, Vol. 4, Apr., 48—82.

Anglo-Saxon Chronicle. Anon., Trans. Anne Savage, Heinemann, London.

BARBER T.W. *The Port of London and the Thames Barrage.* A series of expert studies and reports by the Thames Barrage Committee. Swan Sonneschein, London, 1907.

BONDI H. *London flood barrier.* Report to the Ministry of Housing and Local Government, 1967. Unpublished work.

BOWEN A.J. The tidal regime of the River Thames; long term trends and possible causes. *Phil. Trans. Roy. Soc. Lond.*, 1972, **272**, 187—201.

BUNGE J.H.O. *Dam the Thames.* A plan for a tideless river in London. The Thames Barrage Association, London, 1935.

BUNGE J.H.O. The Thames Barrage scheme and its importance to the London reconstruction plans. *J. Roy. Soc. Arts*, 1945, **XCIII**, No. 4692, 25 May.

CORKAN R.H. *Storm surges in the North Sea.* 1/2 HO Misc. 15072, Washington, DC.

CHURCHILL D.M. The displacement of deposits formed at sea level 6500 years ago in Southern Britain. *Quaternia*, 1965, No. 7, 239.

CREMER and WARNER. *Assessment of the effect on pollution of a full barrage located near London Bridge.* Cremer and Warner, London, 1969.

DEPARTMENT OF SCIENTIFIC AND INDUSTRIAL RESEARCH. Effects of polluting discharges in the Thames Estuary. *Wat. Poll. Res. Tech. Paper 11*, HMSO, London, 1964.

DOODSON A.T. and DINES J.S. Report on Thames floods and meteorological conditions associated with high tides in the Thames. *Geophysical Memoirs No. 47*, 1929.

DOYLE R. *The deluge*. Arlington, 1976, and Pan, London, 1978.

DUNHAM K.C. The evidence for subsidence of South-East England. *Phil. Trans. Roy. Soc. Lond.*, 1972, **A272**, 79–274.

GILBERT S.K. *The Thames Barrage*, Vernon Harcourt Lecture to the Institution of Civil Engineers, 1969.

GRAY D.A. and FOSTER S.S.D. Urban influences on groundwater conditions in the Thames flood plain deposits of Central London. *Phil. Trans. Roy. Soc. Lond.*, 1972, **A272**, 245–257.

GRICE J.R. and HEPPLEWHITE E.A. Design and construction of the Thames Barrier cofferdams. *Proc. Instn Civ. Engrs*, Part 1, 1983, **74**, May, 191–224.

GRIEVE H. *The great tide*. Essex County Council, 1959.

GUMBEL E.J. *Probability tables for the analysis of extreme value data*. US Dept of Commerce, National Bureau of Standards, Applied Mathematics, Series 22, July 1953.

HORNER R.W. The Thames Barrier scheme. *J. Roy. Soc. Arts*, 1971, **CXIX**, No. 5178, May, 369–383.

HORNER R.W. The Thames Barrier. *J. Instn Wat. Engng Sci.*, 1981, **35**, No. 5, 395–407.

HERBERT A.P. *The Thames*. Weidenfeld and Nicolson, London, 1966.

HEAPS N.S. Development of storm surge models at Bidston, *Internal Report No. 51*, Institute of Oceanography, 1977.

INGLIS C.C. and ALLEN F.H. The regimen of the Thames Estuary as affected by currents, salinities and river flow. *Proc. Instn Civ. Engrs*, 1957, **7**, May–Aug., 827–878.

JENKINSON A.F. Frequency distribution of annual maximum (or minimum) values of meteorological elements. *Qu. J. Roy. Met. Soc.*, 1955, **81**, Apr., 158–171.

KEERS J.F. An empirical investigation of interaction between storm surge and astronomical tide on the east coast of Britain. *Conf. on floods due to high winds and tides*. Academic Press, London, 1968.

LONGFIELD T.E. The subsidence of London. *Ordnance Survey Professional Papers, New Series No. 4*, 1932.

MINISTRY OF HOUSING AND LOCAL GOVERNMENT. Technical possibilities of a Thames flood barrier. *Command 956*, HMSO, London, 1960.

MARSH T.J. and DAVIES P.A. *Proc. Instn Civ. Engrs*, Part 1, 1983, **74**, May, 263–276.

MINISTRY OF AGRICULTURE, FISHERIES AND FOOD. *Oceanographic and meteorological research*. First report of the Advisory Committee, HMSO, London, 1962.

North Sea floods of 1953. Conference at the Institution of Civil Engineers, London, 1954.

PARIS M. *Chronica Majora*, **iii**, 1216–1239, Rolls Series, 1876.

PUGH D.T. and VASSIE J.M. Applications of the joint probability method for extreme sea level computations. *Proc. Instn Civ. Engrs*, 1969, **42**, Dec., 959–975.

Report of a committee to consider the question of floods from the River Thames. *Cmd 3045*, HMSO, 1928.

Report of the Departmental Committee on coastal flooding. *Cmd 9165*, HMSO, 1954.

ROBINSON H. On the past and present condition of the River Thames. *Proc. Instn Civ. Engrs*, 1856, **XV**, 205—210.

ROSSITER J.R. Interaction between tide and surge in the Thames. *Geophys. J. R. Astr. Soc.*, 1961, **6**, 29—53.

ROSSITER J.R. and LENNON G.W. An intensive analysis of shallow water tides. *Geophys. J. R. Astr. Soc.*, 1968, **16**, 275—293.

ROSSITER J.R. First report of studies, Thames Flood Prevention Investigation App. 7, Greater London Council, 1969.

ROSSITER J.R. Research on methods of forecasting storm surges on the east and south coasts of Great Britain. *Q. J. R. Met. Soc.*, 1959, **85**, 262—277.

ROTHWELL D. *et al. Management of an urgent public works project*, 1975, School of Technological Management, University of Bradford.

SHELDON H. Excavation at Toppings and Sun Wharves, Southwark 1970—72. *Trans. London and Middlesex Archaeological Society*, 1974, **25**, 1—3.

INSTITUTION OF CIVIL ENGINEERS *et al.* Conditions of contract for works of civil engineering construction.

STOW J. *The Chronicles of England*, 1580.

SOUTH-EAST ECONOMIC PLANNING COUNCIL. *A strategy for the South East. A first report.* HMSO, London, 1967.

SUTHONS C.T. Frequency of occurrence of abnormally high sea levels on the east and south coasts of England. *Proc. Instn Civ. Engrs*, 1963, **25**, 433—449.

Thames Barrier design. Institution of Civil Engineers, London, 1978.

Thames Barrier and Flood Prevention Act 1972. HMSO, London.

Thames Flood Prevention. First Report of Studies. Greater London Council, 1969.

Thames Flood Prevention. Second Report of Studies. Greater London Council, 1970.

TOWNSEND J. Storm surges and their forecasting. *Conf. on floods due to high winds and tides.* IMA, Academic Press, London, 1980.

VALENTIN H. Present vertical movements in the British Isles: *Geog. J.*, 1953, **119**, 229.

WILLCOX G.H. Problems and possible conclusions related to the history and archaeology of the Thames in the London region. *Trans. London and Middlesex Archaeological Society*, 1975, **26**, 285—292.

WOLF J. Surge tide interaction in the North Sea and River Thames. *Conf. on floods due to high winds and tides.* IMA, Academic Press, London, 1980.

Appendix 1. Designs for the Thames Barrier

A variety of designs for the proposed Thames Barrier were submitted in 1953—54 by the Chief Engineers of the various official bodies concerned with the surge tide flooding problem—the Port of London Authority (PLA), the Admiralty, the London County Council, the London riverside boroughs (outside the LCC area), and the river boards. Except where otherwise stated the designs were intended for the site in the middle of Long Reach (alongside the Dartford tunnel); in accordance with the requirements of the PLA they had to comprise two 500 ft openings for shipping and two 250 ft openings for small craft next to the river banks. All these designs were discussed at length by the Thames Technical Panel. Brief descriptions of some of these designs are as follows:

(a) a vast road viaduct from which two 500 ft sluice gates were lowered

(b) two 500 ft hollow concrete caissons similar to those used in the Mulberry Harbour, which would be moored alongside the bank and winched out towards a central dolphin, water being admitted to sink them when in position

(c) two ship caissons, each 500 ft long, of the type used to close the entrances of some modern large dry docks, hinged to abutments in the river bank, and drawn out to a centre pier

(d) two 500 ft openings spanned by a swing bridge from which Venetian type shutters were to be dropped

(e) a shutter lying on and hinged to a sill on the river bed with a toggle jointed strut arrangement to lift and support it

(f) a shutter gate similar to (e), but with tanks into which compressed air could be blown to produce flotation and so raise it

(g) a 1200 ft long caisson swinging about a pivot at its centre, the pivot being fixed in the middle of the river to balance the force of the current when closing

(h) two 500 ft caissons sliding into recesses in the river bank; this is an enlargement of the normal scheme for a wide dry dock entrance, but took no account of the sideways force on the caissons if moved out with a strong current running

(i) similar to (f), a shutter hinged to a sill in the river bed and hinged to a flotation pontoon along the other edge

(j) two 500 ft openings closed by ordinary swinging dock gates which close to the normal mitre formation, the gates operated by cables

(k) shutter gates hinged to the roof of a tunnel and raised by compressed air, but held by chains against tidal pressures

(l) two 400 ft bascule spans which drop like a castle drawbridge; when these had been dropped gates which were stored on shore would be run out hanging from tracks on the bascules

(m) a new channel cut through the Swanscombe Marshes, the barrier (choice of types) built in this in the dry, the Thames then diverted into this channel

(n) two 550 ft gates lying on the river bed; floated up by blowing out tanks with compressed air, into horizontal position; the gates are then turned to the vertical moving about pivots; the pivots have moved up along vertical channels formed in the abutments.

Appendix 2. Two designs for the Crayfordness site

The low-level girder scheme

Rendel Palmer & Tritton proposed to support their girders partly by flotation and partly on giant pneumatic tyres, running on the underwater sill. The lateral forces during launching were minimised by having nothing but the girder structure and flotation tanks below water, the sluice gates when in their open position being entirely above water. Lateral support during launching was obtained by additional pneumatic-tyred wheels turning on vertical axles and bearing against vertical surfaces of the underwater sill. The sluices lie on an inclined plane so that water pressure on them has a downward as well as a lateral component. When they close the force on them is transmitted to the concrete sill by bringing the girder into direct contact with a suitably inclined concrete surface. This is done simply, but with considerable ingenuity, by allowing both sets of giant pneumatic tyres on the upstream side of the girder to be squashed down by a matter of 4 inches by the force of the water acting on the inclined sluices, a device, infallible in action, and costing nothing.

The primary requirement for the barrier after 1961 was to offer an unobstructed channel for navigation 1400 ft wide. As the river at the selected site is wider than this, and as an increase in length of a structure of this nature was not limited by a requirement for increased restraining forces at its end (as is the case in the high-level scheme), the low-level girder was designed to give an opening of 1600 ft.

The girders are normally housed in dry docks; each is 850 ft long. They will be supported by keel blocks on the dock bottom, and the support of the keel blocks will not be withdrawn until the docks are flooded ready for barrier operation. Most of the weight of the girder will then be taken by flotation tanks built into its structure. The remainder of the weight of the girder will rest on the 164 wheels fitted with giant pneumatic tyres of about 5 ft diameter. These will run on concrete tracks formed in the under-river sills. The girder will be guided laterally, and constrained against the force of the river current to run along the tracks by the second set of wheels, also fitted with pneumatic tyres, which are mounted horizontally underneath the girder in such a position that they will

157

bear against surfaces formed in the sill.

The girder structure is 70 ft high and 77 ft wide. The sluice gates are set into its framework at an angle of 45° so that the pressure of water on them, when they close, will press the girder backwards and downwards. The girder and the concrete track are both provided with suitably inclined faces which come into contact.

The girders would be run out and retracted by cables led from winch houses at the inner ends of the dry docks. The haulage ropes act through a haulage girder which spans the dry dock at the rear of the barrier girder and runs on tracks fixed to the dry dock walls.

Extending the plane of the sluice gates, and closing the area above them to the surge, are hinged flap valves. These open automatically as soon as the height of the water on the landward side of the barrier exceeds that of the outgoing tide on its seaward side. These valves prevent a build-up of pressure on the wrong side of the barrier.

This simplicity in construction of the barrier girders is bought at the cost of special arrangements to take care of two adverse factors: the girder cannot move across the sill if silt, debris or small craft and so on are lying on it; and the concrete tracks across the sill must be constructed to an accuracy of less than an inch for line and level, the construction being carried out under water. The girder will be provided with very powerful water jets at its leading end to remove silt, and massive ploughblades to push away anything in the nature of anchors or small craft which may have sunk on the sill.

The designer's solution for constructing an underwater sill in which the wheel tracks should be so accurate is elaborate. A trench is to be dredged in the river bed about 100 ft wide at the bottom and 30 ft (or perhaps a little more) deep. With inclined sides dredged at a slope at which they will stand under water this trench might be 200—220 ft wide at the top. Concrete piles are driven in the bottom of the trench so arranged that they will act as seats on which to place precast sill units. After the concrete piles have been driven, and then cut off to leave stumps somewhat below the required level, there are special arrangements for casting new heads on them to reach the correct level. This is done under water by grouting inside a nylon sleeve.

Special concrete sill units each 91 ft long, 108 ft wide and 27 ft deep are now constructed at some convenient point, such as a dry dock from which they can be floated to the barrier site. These sill units are something like egg boxes, each having 80 rectangular cells open at the top and bottom except for those round the periphery, which are closed at the bottom to assist flotation. The cells are separated by walls about 1 ft thick. The concrete tracks on which the wheels of the girder will run are formed in these units. A projection is made in what will be the mid-river or leading edge of the unit when laid, which will engage with a recess in the trailing edge of the next laid unit.

At the same time as these sill units are being made the girder will be built in the dry dock, but omitting its leading sections over a length of more than 100 ft. A false nose, about 100 ft long, will then be bolted temporarily to the leading end of the girder. This false nose will have its top members in continuation of the upper members of the girder, but its lower members leave a clearance sufficient to allow a sill unit to be floated underneath it.

The false nose is fitted with four sets of lifting tackle which will enable it to pick up a sill unit. The false nose is also fitted with four spuds which have a length sufficient to enable them to be lowered to the bottom of the dredged trench. These spuds (vertical legs with feet) are so located that with a sill unit properly lined up under the false nose the spuds will pass through four of the open cells and act as rigid guides when the unit is being lowered into position.

The first sill unit is floated under the false nose. Part of the flotation would be provided by the closed compartments of the sill unit and part by the use of 'camels' (flotation units). The girder is moved out, carrying the sill unit under its false nose, until the unit is directly above the position in which it is to be laid. The sill unit is then dropped on to its seating. The recess in the trailing end of the unit will engage with and seat on the projection in the leading end of the previously laid unit. The leading end of the unit will come down on to jacks placed on the pile caps of the next set of piles. The final adjustment for line and level will be made with these jacks which are subsequently concreted in.

A lattice steel mast fixed to the leading end of each sill unit projects above the top of the girder. The tip of the mast will be lined up between sighting stations on the two banks of the river to ensure that the front end of the unit (which will, at this stage, be deeply under water) is correctly positioned for line and level. The trailing end of the unit will have been correctly positioned by the engagement of its recess with the projection on the unit previously laid.

When the 'egg box' sill unit has been fixed in position in this way the girder will be withdrawn into its dry dock and a concreting plant mounted on a barge and provided with tremie pipes will pour concrete through each of the cells so that it fills the space between the unit and the bottom of the trench, fills all the cells solid, and also fills the space between the unit and the sides of the trench.

The sill will rise at a gradient of 1 in 100 from the centre of the river, where its level is −45 ft OD(N) towards the banks. The level at the dock entrances will be −37 ft OD(N) and at the inner ends of the docks −28 ft OD(N).

The dry docks will be 1000 ft long, 100 ft wide and 67 ft deep. They will have walls of heavy box section sheet steel piling. The tops of the sheet piling will be tied into box section reinforced concrete members 40 ft wide and 12 ft deep. These will carry dockside crane tracks and roadways. They will themselves be supported by reinforced concrete piles, inclined to resist the earth pressure acting against the sheet piling. The dock floor will be 10 ft thick, tied down against uplift by reinforced concrete anchor piles. The dock gates will be sliding caissons.

It will be noted that the operation of a barrier of this type, after the dry docks have been flooded and their gates opened, will simply be to run it out across the river and then close the sluice gates.

Great care will have to be taken to ensure that any material accidentally falling on the sill is removed. This will involve frequent underwater inspection. The consulting engineers have suggested a type of diving bell from which there is constant access to the surface. Either the normal air-hose-equipped divers, frogmen, underwater television or a combination of some of these would be required for inspection. Water or air jetting would remove silt, whilst light salvage equipment would remove debris. Such equipment would be available at the barrier site. If a craft sank on the sill heavy salvage equipment would be summoned from elsewhere in the Thames.

The high-level girder scheme

Sir Bruce White, Wolfe Barry and Partners considered it desirable that the girders forming the framework of the barrier should move across the river at a height above the sill level which would enable them to pass over small craft, debris or silt which might be lying on the sill. If such objects were on the sill it might not be possible to close those sections of the barrier where they lay completely down upon the sill, but it would be possible to close all the other sections completely and probably to close the obstructed sections in a large measure. The barrier would still fulfil its function of protecting London even if leakage of the order of a spring tide ran past it, so that partial closure of some sections would not invalidate the barrier's function.

Although the girder was to move into position at a high level, arrangements had to be made by which the whole of the lateral pressure of the water would be transmitted direct to the concrete sill. In this way the girder would only have to be designed to withstand the forces imposed on it during launching. However, owing to the immense length of the overhang, 700 ft, these forces proved to be very large.

Three ways were found of reducing them. The weight of the barrier units which seal the gap between the underside of the girder and the sill was reduced by making them of aluminium. The weight of the girder itself was reduced by the use of high tensile steel, and a large part of the girder's weight was arranged to be supported by flotation. Even so, each girder is a massive structure 1126 ft long, 90 ft high and 120 ft wide. The bottom of the girder is formed by the flotation tank, which extends over its full width and for a depth of 8 ft. The top of this tank is at −6 ft OD(N) so that at most stages of the tide when the barrier is in operation it will be entirely submerged, thus minimising changes in the uplift due to flotation. The space above the tank top up to the maximum design flood level of 23 ft OD(N) can be closed by vertical sluice gates.

The key to the action of this design lies in the triangular barrier units. They are wedge shaped, 70 ft long where they lie across the sill and standing 40 ft high from the sill to their pivot. The cross river dimension is also 40 ft. The pivots at the upper edge of the barrier unit turn in eyes in the ends of link bars, 65 ft long. The other end of the link bar is pivoted in the centre of the girder just above the deck of the flotation chamber. The position of the link bar is controlled by a vertical hydraulic cylinder attached to the seaward face of the girder which can raise that end of the link bar, and hence the pivot of the barrier unit by about 15 ft. The outer end of the barrier unit can be raised by chain cables which pass over sheaves in the top of the seaward face of the girder, and from those to hydraulic winches located in the top of the structure. These chain cables will be made with links of parallel flat plates.

When the barrier unit is lowered its 'heel' will come back against a steel abutment built into the concrete sill. The downward force of the water on the inclined face of the barrier unit will ensure a contact between its heel and the abutment which will transmit the lateral force of the water on the barrier unit and also, acting through the 65 ft link, the lateral force on the girder, directly to the sill.

The sill itself is rectangular in cross section 210 ft wide by 30 ft deep of solid concrete. It would be constructed by dredging a trench, mixing the concrete on a barge located by spud legs, and pouring the concrete down tremie pipes. This

160

arrangement fulfils the condition that there should, during the building of the barrier, be no obstruction in the river that cannot be moved as readily as a dredger.

The girders are housed in dry docks. These are 1140 ft by 220 ft by 43 ft deep. The floors are 20 ft thick, the landward walls are of reinforced concrete, the seaward walls are sloped to enable the barrier units to be partially lowered whilst the girder is in the dry dock. Each dock is provided with a Goliath crane spanning 245 ft and standing 120 ft above the dockside rails on which it runs. These rails and the associated dockside service roads are supported on long reinforced concrete piles. The dry docks are provided with sliding caisson gates. The girders rest on hydraulically operated keel blocks, which can lower them on to 4 ft diameter steel rollers in the bottom of the docks prior to running out. When resting on the rollers part of the weight will be supported by flotation.

When the girder emerges from the dry dock into the tidal current there will be a strong side pressure on it. This pressure is transmitted through steel rollers to a massive portal at the dry dock entrance. This has batteries of rollers on its lower surface, beneath its transom and on both of its inner vertical faces. These rollers rest on hydraulic jacks which equalise the pressures between them, and can also be used to lift the girder or move it laterally.

When the girder has run out about 260 ft beyond the dock entrance portal it passes on to a pier set in the river, and after adjustment of position by the jacks at the dock entrance, it passes on to a battery of steel rollers on the pier, and between buttress walls, whose inner faces are likewise furnished with rollers. These piers are massive constructions 520 ft long, 93 ft wide and 100 ft high, set across the river sill. They take the vertical and lateral reactions from the girder as it passes outwards across the current for its 700 ft cantilever length. These reaction forces are as follows:

	Horizontal	Vertical
At the dock entrances	1300 tons	4400 tons
At the river piers	2700 tons	15 500 tons

(The 15 500 t weight coming on to the 4 ft diameter rollers of the river pier is probably larger than anything else designed to move on wheels.)

The girders are hauled in and out of the dry docks by cables led to out haul winches located on top of the dock entrance portals and back haul winches located on the other ends of the dry docks.

The various powered operations on the girder, the operation of the upper sluice gates, the adjustment of the height of the 65 ft links, and the lifting winches for the barrier units, will all be operated hydraulically, and it is intended that the pumps for this purpose would be mounted on the girders. The maximum load on the lifting winches for the central barrier unit is 1500 tons, just before the unit touches down on the sill. The hydraulic machinery would therefore be on a massive scale, requiring about 3500 h.p. for each girder.

Dimensions

The vast dimensions of the two schemes are compared below:

	High-level barrier	Low-level barrier
Clear navigational opening	1400 ft	1600 ft
Length of each of the two girders	1126 ft	850 ft
Width of girder	120 ft	77 ft
Height of girder	91 ft	70 ft
Length of each dry dock	1140 ft	900 ft
Width	220 ft	100 ft
Depth	43 ft	67 ft

(If we imagine one of the girders of the high-level design laid down in Whitehall it would reach from Parliament Square to the Horse Guards. It would fill the full width of the street and would extend well above the buildings. The dry docks for the high-level scheme would take a 200 000 t vessel. Those for the low-level scheme would admit the Queen Elizabeth 2 even at low tide.)

The power required to operate these vast moving structures is very large. For the high-level barrier it is:

(a) four winches for each girder	5200 h.p.
(b) hydraulic pumps for jacks controlling rollers	400 h.p.
(c) the hydraulic pumps serving the rams and winches controlling the barrier units and sluice gates	7000 h.p.
(d) dewatering pumps for the dry docks	4200 h.p.
(e) other powered installations	1000 h.p.
Approximate total installation	17800 h.p.

The maximum simultaneous power demand would be about 7000 h.p.
The power required for the low-level barrier is approximately:

(a) four winches for each girder	4000 h.p.
(b) silt jetting pumps	800 h.p.
(c) hydraulic operation of girder sluices	600 h.p.
(d) dewatering pumps for the dry docks	4000 h.p.
(e) other powered installations	1000 h.p.
Approximate total installation	10 400 h.p.

The maximum simultaneous power demand would be about 5000 h.p.

The Consulting Engineers have estimated for a connection to the national grid and for stand-by diesel generators. In this connection it is always possible that abnormal weather conditions capable of damaging electricity supply lines might accompany a surge tide.

Cost estimates

	High-level scheme, £	Low-level scheme, £
Consulting Engineers' estimates (1965)	39 000 000	23 000 000
Other items	2 250 000	1 550 000
Total capital expenditure	41 250 000	24 550 000

Appendix 3. Members of committees

Policy Committee		
Eldon Griffiths (Chairman 1970 on)	Parliamentary Secretary	Department of the Environment
Lord Kennet (Chairman 1968–70)	Former Joint Parliamentary Secretary	Ministry of Housing and Local Government
R.C. Chilver	Deputy Secretary	Department of the Environment
J.E. Beddoe	Under Secretary	
W.J. Glenn	Chief Engineer	
B.C. Wood	Deputy Chief Engineer	
R.G. Adams	Assistant Secretary	
J.E. Sanderson	Assistant Secretary	(ex Ministry of Transport)
Col S.K. Gilbert	Engineering Inspector	
B.M. Baker		
A. Savage	Assistant Secretary	Ministry of Agriculture, Fisheries and Food
E.A.G. Johnson	Chief Engineer	
E.R. Hargreaves	Assistant Secretary	Department of Trade and Industry
Capt. H. Menzies	Professional Officer Marine Division, Branch 3A	
R.C.H. Russell	Director (Chief Scientific Officer)	Hydraulics Research Station
Mrs M. Kendrick	Senior Scientific Officer	
B. Derbyshire	Experimental Officer	
J.F. Stanbury	Chief Engineer	Port of London Authority
Capt. G.R. Rees	River Manager	
J.H. Potter	River Conservator	

Capt. J.E. Bury	Elder Brother (Chairman of Pilotage Committee)	Corporation of Trinity House
Rear Adm. P.W.W. Graham	Head of Radio and Navigation Department	Chamber of Shipping of the United Kingdom
S.H.J. Bates	Chairman	Essex River Authority
G.L. Sturgess	Clerk	
E.L. Snell	Engineer	
J. Mason	Chairman	Kent River Authority
H. Catt	Vice Chairman	
J.I. Taylor	Engineer	
P. Black	Chairman, Public Services Committee 1968—70	Greater London Council
M.P. Gaffney	Chairman, Public Services Committee 1970—71	
Lt Col. A. Jardine	Vice Chairman, Public Services Committee	
W.L. Hooper	Assistant Director General	
S.H. Dainty	Director, Public Health Engineering	
A.C. Darlow	Deputy Director (Management Services)	
R.W. Horner	Project Manager	
P.G.D. Shallow	Deputy Project Manager	
Dr B.R. Brown	Scientific Advisor	

Steering Committee

S.H. Dainty (Chairman)	Director	GLC Department of Public Health Engineering
A.C. Darlow	Deputy Director (Management Services)	
R.W. Horner	Project Manager	
W.L. Hooper	Assistant Director General	GLC Director General's Department
B.C. Wood	Deputy Chief Engineer	Department of the Environment
Col S.K. Gilbert	Engineering Inspector	
E.A.G. Johnson	Chief Engineer	Ministry of Agriculture, Fisheries and Food
K.C. Noble	Senior Engineer	
E.R. Hargreaves	Assistant Secretary	Department of Trade and Industry
Capt. H. Menzies	Professional Officer, Marine Division, Branch 3A	

Mrs M. Kendrick	Senior Scientific Officer	Hydraulics Research Station
J.F. Stanbury	Chief Engineer	Port of London Authority
Capt. G.R. Rees	River Manager	
J.H. Potter	River Conservator	
Lt Cdr P.F.C. Satow	River Superintendent	
Rear Adm. P.W.W. Graham	Head of Radio and Navigation Department	Chamber of Shipping of the United Kingdom
D. Deacon	Secretary, Navigation Panel	
Capt. J.T. Gibson	Chairman, Navigation Panel	
J.I. Taylor	Engineer	Kent River Authority
E.L. Snell	Engineer	Essex River Authority
Capt. J.E. Bury	Elder Brother (Chairman of Pilotage Committee)	Corporation of Trinity House
Cdr G.G. Greenfield	River Thames Pilot	
F. Stanyard	Assistant Treasurer, E Branch	GLC Treasurer's Department
D.G. Ball	Principal Clerk	
Dr B.R. Brown	Scientific Advisor	GLC Director General's Department (Scientific)
L.B. Wood	Assistant Scientific Advisor	
H.W. Fulton	Principal Clerk	GLC Legal and Parliamentary Department

---

Navigation Working Party

R.W. Horner (Chairman)	Project Manager	GLC Department of Public Health Engineering
P.G.D. Shallow	Deputy Project Manager	
R.A.B. Hall	Professional Officer	
Col S.K. Gilbert	Engineering Inspector	Department of the Environment
Capt. H. Menzies	Professional Officer Marine Division, Branch 3A	Department of Trade and Industry
E.R. Hargreaves	Assistant Secretary	

Capt. G.R. Rees	River Manager	Port of London
J.H. Potter	River Conservator	Authority
Lt Cdr P.F.C. Satow	River Superintendent	

Capt. J.T. Gibson	Chairman, Navigation Panel	Chamber of Shipping of the United Kingdom
D. Deacon	Secretary, Navigation Panel	
Capt. H.J. Hayes	Manager, Ship Management Department, Shell Mex and BP	

| Capt. J.E. Bury | Elder Brother (Chairman of Pilotage Committee) | Corporation of Trinity House |
| Cdr G.G. Greenfield | River Thames Pilot | |

| A.H. Beckett | Partner | Sir Bruce White, Wolfe |
| W.A. Barton | Project Engineer | Barry & Partners |

| H. Scrutton | Partner | Rendel, Palmer & |
| A.R. Young | Senior Engineer | Tritton |

| Capt. D.T. Scanes | Marine Superintendent | GLC Department of Mechanical and Electrical Engineering |

Oceanographical and Meteorological Working Party

R.W. Horner (Chairman)	Project Manager	GLC Department of
P.G.D. Shallow	Deputy Project Manager	Public Health
B. Hall	Research Engineer	Engineering

| Cdr C.T. Suthons RN (Ret'd) | | Formerly Hydrographic Department, Admiralty |

| Dr J.R. Rossiter | Director | Institute of Coastal Oceanography and Tides |

| Col S.K. Gilbert | Engineering Inspector | Department of the Environment |

| K.C. Noble | Senior Engineer | Ministry of Agriculture, Fisheries and Food |

| J.S. Sawyer | Director of Research | Meteorological Office |

| Mrs M. Kendrick | Senior Scientific Officer | Hydraulics Research Station |

Pollution and Siltation Working Party

R.W. Horner (Chairman)	Project Manager	GLC Department of
P.G.D. Shallow	Deputy Project Manager	Public Health
B. Hall	Research Engineer	Engineering
R.E. Beardsall	Professional Officer	
Col S.K. Gilbert	Engineering Inspector	Department of the
T. Waldmeyer	Chemical Inspector	Environment
J.H. Potter	River Conservator	Port of London Authority
Mrs M. Kendrick	Senior Scientific Officer	Hydraulics Research Station
A.L.H. Gameson	Principal Scientific Officer	Water Pollution
M.J. Barrett	Senior Experimental Officer	Research Laboratory
Dr D. Train	Partner	Cremer and Warner
K.M. Gammon	Group Head, (South East)	Central Electricity
I. Davies	Divisional Head	Generating Board
W.E. Foster	Deputy Chief Engineer	Thames Conservancy
L.B. Wood	Assistant Scientific Advisor	GLC Director General's Department (Scientific)

Groundwater Effects Working Party

R.W. Horner (Chairman)	Project Manager	GLC Department of
P.G.D. Shallow	Deputy Project Manager	Public Health
B. Hall	Research Engineer	Engineering
Col S.K. Gilbert	Engineering Inspector	Department of the Environment
D.A. Gray	Chief Hydrogeologist	Institute of Geological
S.S.D. Foster	Senior Scientific Officer	Sciences
A. Marsland	Principal Scientific Officer	Building Research Station
B.J. Hardcastle	Water Resources Engineer	Thames Conservancy
Dr J. Ineson	Chief Geologist	Water Resources Board

Engineering Working Party

R.W. Horner (Chairman)	Project Manager	GLC Department of
P.G.D. Shallow	Deputy Project Manager	Public Health
E.H. Adams	Professional Officer	Engineering
R.A.B. Hall	Professional Officer	
Col S.K. Gilbert	Engineering Inspector	Department of the Environment
J.F. Stanbury	Director of Engineering	Port of London
F.A. Page	Design Engineer	Authority
R.E. West	Assistant Engineer (Design)	
A.H. Beckett	Partner	Sir Bruce White, Wolfe
W.A. Barton	Project Engineer	Barry and Partners
H. Scrutton	Partner	Rendel Palmer &
A.R. Young	Senior Engineer	Tritton
Dr J.D. Hardwick	Lecturer	Imperial College of Science and Technology
R.H. Arbuckle	Assistant Director	GLC Department of
B.H. Fordham	Divisional Engineer, Electrical Power Division	Mechanical and Electrical Engineering
N. Barnes	Assistant Divisional Engineer, Electrical Power Division	
R.S. Thompson	Professional Officer	

Amenity Working Party

R.W. Horner (Chairman)	Project Manager	GLC Department of
P.G.D. Shallow	Deputy Project Manager	Public Health
B. Hall	Research Engineer	Engineering
Col S.K. Gilbert	Engineering Inspector	Department of the Environment
W.L. Hooper	Assistant Director General	GLC Director General's Department
M. Hennings	Planning Architect	GLC Department of
E.J.L. Griffith	Assistant Group Planning Officer, Strategy Branch	Planning and Transportation
M.G. Hudson	Professional Officer, Transportation Branch	

M.S. Hodgson	Assistant Group Planning Officer, Plans Branch	
L.W. Franklin	Head of Entertainments Division	GLC Parks Department
L.G. Whiteman	Administrative Officer	GLC Treasurer's Department

Appendix 4. Thames Barrier contracts

Contract No.	Contract description	Main Contractor
1A	Dredging initial diversion channel to provide northern navigation route	Kier-Broekhoven
1B	Maintenance dredging of diversion channel, 1975/6	Westminster Dredging
1C	Interim maintenance dredging	Westminster Dredging
2A	Preliminary works (1),—fencing demolition, and diversion of services	H. Smith, Orpington
2B	Preliminary works (2),—approach roads, site accommodation, river wall, and associated work	J. Mowlem
3	Main civil works, concrete piers and abutments, gate sills, river walls, and associated work	Costain/Tarmac/HBM Joint Venture
4A	Trunnion shaft support structures (supply and delivery only)	Voest Alpine A.G.
4B	Trunnion shafts (supply and delivery only)	British Steel Corporation
4C	Special bearings (supply and delivery only)	Merriman Inc.

4D	Operating machinery (manufacture, supply, delivery, installation and maintenance)	Davy/Cleveland Barrier Consortium
5A	Onshore works; control tower, generator building, workshop and sub-stations	Sindall Construction
6	Steel gates (manufacture, supply, delivery and installation)	Davy Cleveland Barrier Consortium
7A	Diesel generators	Mirrlees Blackstone
7B	High-voltage switchgear and transformers	GEC Distribution Switchgear
7C	Control panels and equipment	Henry Williams
7D	Mechanical and electrical services	Balfour Kilpatrick
7E	Local control panels	British Brown Boveri
7F	Low-voltage switchgear	Sunderland Forge
7G	Lifts	Evans Lifts
7H	Navigation lights	Aga (UK)
8A	South bank ancillary works	J. Mowlem

Appendix 5. Downriver contracts

Authority and Contract Designation	Main Contractor
Greater London Council	
Flood walls Contract 9	Kier
Flood walls Contract 10	Howard
Flood walls Contract 11	Christiani & Nielsen
Flood walls Contract 12	Holland, Hannen & Cubitts
Flood walls Contract 13	Nuttall
Flood walls Contract 14	French-Kier
Flood walls Contract 15	French-Kier
Flood walls Contract 16	Howard
Flood walls Contract 17	Dredging & Construction
Flood walls Contract 18	Costain
Flood walls Contract 19	Laing
Flood walls Contract 20A	Mowlem
Flood walls Contract 20B	Mowlem
Floodgate Royal Docks 21	Adamson & Butterley
Flood walls Contract 21A	Peter Birse
Flood walls Contract 21B	Peter Birse
Floodgate PLA impounding culvert, Contract 21C	Armfield
Floodgate Lower Gallion's Lock, Contract 21D	Tinsley Moulds Ltd
Flood walls Contract 23A	Laing
Flood walls Contract 24	Dawson
Flood walls Contract 25	Nuttall
Flood walls Contract 26	Fairclough
Southern Water Authority	
Dartford Creek Barrier, civil work	Howard
Dartford Creek Barrier, gates and machinery	RDL

Flood walls, lengths 3A and 4A, stage 1	Kier Broekhoven
Flood walls, length 4B	Laing
Flood walls, lengths 3 and 4, stage 2	Laing
Flood walls, lengths 3 and 4, stage 3	Crownway Construction
Flood walls, lengths 5/1–3	Howard
Flood walls, lengths 5/4–7	French-Kier
Flood walls, length 5/8	Kier
Flood walls, length 5/9	Laing
Flood walls, lengths 5/10–11	Nuttall-Mears
Flood walls, lengths 5/12–13	Nuttall-Mears
Flood walls, length 5/14	Higgs & Hill
Flood walls, length 7A, stage 1	Tilbury
Flood walls, length 7B, stage 1	Westminster Dredging
Flood walls, length 8A, stage 1	Westminster Dredging
Flood walls, lengths 7 and 8, stage 2	Laing
Flood walls, lengths 7 and 8, stage 3	Laing
Flood walls, length 8, Higham counterwall	Peter Birse
Flood walls, length 9	Peter Birse
Flood walls, length 10	Peter Birse
Flood walls, length 11	Peter Birse
Thames and Anglian Water Authorities	
Flood walls, Contract 11	Dawson
Flood walls, Contract 12	Sir Robert McAlpine
Flood walls, Contract 13A, stage 1	Costain
Flood walls, Contract 13/2, stage 2	Dawson
Flood walls, Contract 14	Mowlem
Flood walls, Contract 14/1	Lilley
Flood walls, Contract 14/4	Dawson
Flood walls, Contract 15	Mears
Flood walls, Contract 15/1	Costain
Flood walls, Contract 15/4	Land & Marine
Flood walls, Contract 17/1	Laing
Flood walls, Contract 17/2	Kier
Flood walls, Contract 17/3	Dawson
Sheet piling, Contract 18/5	Dawson
Sheet piling, Contract 18/6	Dawson
Flood walls, Contract 18/7	Nuttall-Mears
Flood walls, Contract 19/2	Tilbury Construction
Barking Barrier, Contract 20B, civil works	French-Kier
Barking Barrier, Contract 20E, gates and machinery	Newton Chambers
Fobbing Horse and Easthaven Barriers, Contract 21	Howard

Floodgates Barking and Dagenham, Contract 23/1	Armfield
Floodgates Tilbury, Contract 23/2	Newton Chambers
Floodgates Purfleet to Grays, Contract 23/3	Armfield
Flood walls, Contract 24	RDL
Benfleet Barrier, Contract 25	Nuttall-Mears
Floodgate, Tilbury Docks	Cleveland Bridge

This table of downstream contracts is reproduced from the Thames Barrier Supplement (November 1982) by courtesy of Construction News Special Publications Unit, International Thompson Publishing Ltd.

Index

Adams, Richard, 49
Admiralty
  Hydrographer, 24
  Hydrographic Department, 52, 59
Adriatic, 147
AEI, 81
Aga (UK) Ltd, 129
air lift pumps, 98
Amenity Working Party, 84
Anderson, Sir John, 24
Anglo-Saxon Chronicle, 2,
Antwerp, 33, 46
architecture of the barrier, 88, 149
arrester gear, 62
assembly trials, 125
Avon Rubber Co., 78
Ayres, D., 101, 105

Balfour Kilpatrick & Co. Ltd, 129
Baltic, 147
Barking Creek, 130,132
barrage, 57
  Clacton to Herne Bay, 41
  definition, 25
  Gravesend, 7
  half tide, 41
barrier, 25, 27, 30, 57
  Act, 90
  architecture, 149
  Bill, 90
  closure, 134, 142
  Controller, 136
  cost, 141
  definition, 25
  investigation of GLC, 57
  operation, 134
Barrier Project Study Team, 59, 68
Barry, W., 32

bearings
  lubrite, 127
  main, 125
Beckett, A., 40
Beckton, 91
Belgium, 34
Bermondsey, 130
Berry, Henry, Ltd, 115
Birdsell, B., 110
Black, Peter, 58
Blackwall Reach, 61
Board of Trade, 61
Bolton, S., 58
bolts, Monel, 120
Bondi, Professor Sir Hermann, 46, 57, 140,
    145, 146
Bow, 130
Bow Creek, 78
Bow Creek Barrier, 80
Bracknell, 136
Branagen, J., 58
Bray, R., 90
bridge
  built in conjunction with Barrier, 148
  London, 1, 5, 63, 68, 91, 149
  Tower, 44, 66, 75, 149
Bristol University, 89
British Brown Boveri Ltd, 129
British Hydromechanics Research
    Association (BHRA), 38
British Steel Corporation, 125
Broadbent, U., 106
Brook Partridge, B., 105
Brown, C., 133
Bruce White, Wolfe Barry and Partners, 32,
    39, 64
Bubbers, H., 133
building control, 128

Building Research Centre, 63
Bull's Point, 80
Burgess, J.S., 87

Caffin Ltd, 78
Cannon St, 61, 71
Canvey Island, 56, 69, 80
Carr, G., 80
Cassidy, B., 58
Central Electricity Generating Board
    (CEGB), 62, 65
central river fender, 95
chalk, 82
Chamber of Shipping, 58, 61, 75
Charlton, 84
Chiswick, 65
Clacton to Herne Bay Barrage, 41
Cliffe Marshes, 69, 130
Cockerill, 124
Cole, G., 102, 106
Colley, H., 133
Consulting Engineers, 32, 64
container revolution, 45
container terminal, 45
contract plan, 89
contracts
    civil engineering (contract 3), 89, 93
    downstream bank, 132
control tower, 81, 89
Corkan, R.H., 135
Costain Ltd, 93
County Hall, 20,
Cox, Peter, 101
Crayfordness, 37, 72, 91, 140, 145
    design for, 39
    site, 29
Cremer and Warner, 63
critical path network, 78
Crossness, 91
Cubitts Ltd, 78

Dagenham Dock, 57
Dainty, S., 58
damage by flooding, 21
Darlington, 111
Davies, G., 100
Davies, N., 58
Darlow, C., 93
Dartford Creek, 130, 132, 133
Davy Cleveland Barrier Consortium, 110,
    111
Deluge (a novel), 53
designs
    fabric, 54
    outside bodies, 31
Dickens, W., 90, 94
Didcot, 65
Dines, J., 134
diversion channel, 91, 94

docks
    Dagenham, 57
    India and Millwall, 7, 57
    London, 7, 146
    Royal, 45, 101, 130
    St Katharine, 7, 45
    Surrey Commercial, 7, 62, 75
    Tilbury, 45, 130
    West India, 7, 57
Doodson, A., 134
Dowling, Dr P.J., 85
Doyle, Richard, 53
Draper, C., 81
dredging, 7, 16,
    northern diversion channel, 82
drop gate, 34, 72
drum gate, 72
Dunbar, 135
Duty Barrier Controller, 136

East Coast Tide Warning Service, 134
Edwards, A., 58
Eider, River, 51
eight hour shifts, 102
electricity generating stations, 20
emergencies, government reaction to, 141
Engineering Working Party, 64
Erith, 130
Essex marshes, 80
Essex River Authority, 58, 67
Evans Lifts Ltd, 129

fabric sheet dam, 54
Fair Isle, 135
Farquharson, Cmdr W.W.I., 42
finite element analysis, 85
Fire Brigade, 20,
First Report of Studies, 60, 72, 77
Fletcher, J., 122
flood defence levels, 28
    raising of, 28
flood season, 78
flood zone, 9
floods
    1928, 4
    1953, 4, 17
Fobbing Horse, 130
Ford Works, 57
Foundation Engineering Ltd, 82
Franklin, A., 110
Fulton, H., 90

Gaffney, M., 58
Gallions Reach, 80
gasworks, 20,
gate
    construction, 111
    drop, 34, 72
    drum, 72

end placing, 118
placing, 122
rising sector, 81
storage, 120
transport, 117
gate house, 128
General Electric Co. (GEC), 129
generators, diesel, 128, 136
geophysical studies, 84
Gilbert, Col. S.K., 63
Gordon, H., 94
Grainger, R., 94
Greater London Council, 31, 51, 57, 148
    barrier investigation, 57
    Department of Architecture and Civic
        Design, 64, 88
    Department of Mechanical and Electrical
        Engineers, 61
    Department of Planning and Trans-
        portation, 64, 78
    Parks Department, 64
    Public Information Branch, 66
    Treasurer's Department, 64, 102
    Valuation Department, 61
Greenfield, Cmdr G.G.I., 61
Greenwich, 43, 44, 79
Grice, J., 102, 109
Griffiths, Eldon, 49
groundwater, 13, 63, 143

Halfway Reach, 61, 91
Hall, B., 64, 78, 94
Hamburg, 17, 21, 68, 139, 147
Hammersmith, 24
handover arrangements, 103
Hart, C., 129
Hayes, Sir Brian, 50
Health and Safety at Work Act, 142
heavy lift cranes, 118, 122
Hepplewhite, A., 100
Herbert, A.P., 50
Holland, 4
Hollandsche Beton Maatschappij (HBM), 93
Holloway, J., 94, 133
Horner, Ray, 64, 90
House of Commons Committee, 90, 147
Houses of Parliament, 4, 20, 79
Humber, estuary, 130
Hurlingham Club, 79
Hurst, Dr H.E., 42
hydraulic cylinders, 114
Hydraulics Research Station (HRS), 26, 32,
    65, 87, 91
hydroelectric power, 149
Hydrographers Department of the
    Admiralty, 135

Institute of Coastal Oceanography and
    Tides (ICOT), 59

Ijssel, River, 33
Immingham, 135
Imperial College, 121
India and Millwall Docks, 57, 75
industrial disputes, 101, 103, 142
inflatable fabric dam, 54
inflation, 141
Inspectorate of Engineering (MHLG), 31
Institute of Geological Sciences (IGS), 82
Institute of Oceanographic Sciences (IOS),
    135
Institute of Oceanography, 25
Institution of Civil Engineers (ICE), 32
Ineson, Dr J.,
Isle of Dogs, 53

James, D., 90
Jardine, A., 58
Johnson, E., 26, 75, 76
Johnstone, I., 106
joint consulting engineers, 64

Kennet, Lord, 49, 58
Kent marshes, 80
Kent River Authority, 58, 67
Kier Ltd, 78
Kier Broekhoven, 94
Kingston upon Hull, 130

labour agreement, 1979, 103, 108
Lamb, Dr, 59
Lambeth Bridge, 91
Lane, A., 26, 50
Larssen piles, 97
Lee Conservancy Catchment Board (LCCB),
    78
Leningrad, 147
Liège, 124
lift bridge design, 34
lights, navigation, 129
Limehouse, 43
Limehouse Cut, 78
Lind Ltd, 78
Littlebrook Power Station, 84
Liverpool Tidal Institute, 24, 25, 67, 134
load factor, 86
local authorities, participation, 24, 67
London Bridge, 1, 5, 63, 68, 91, 149
London County Council (LCC), 24
Long Reach, 25, 27, 57, 139, 145
Longworth, A., 105
low productivity, 142
Lower Pool, 91

Maisey, W., 122
Maryon Park, 84
Mascall, A., 79, 94
mathematical model, 32, 67
McAlpine, Sir R., 93

179

McCartney, H., 90
Mears Bros, 78
Medway conference, 130
Medway profile, 130
Merriman Inc., 114, 127
Meteorological Office, 24, 52, 134, 135
Metropolis Management (Thames River
    Prevention of Floods) Amendment Act
    (1879) 1B, 23
Metropolitan Board of Works, 23
M1 motorway, 139
micropalaeontological studies, 84
Miller Richards, G., 86
Minister of Agriculture, Fisheries and Food,
    104
Ministry of Agriculture, Fisheries and Food
    (MAFF), 25, 26, 59, 93
Ministry of Defence (MoD), 20
Ministry of Health (MoH), 23
Ministry of Housing and Local Government
    (MHLG), 26, 57, 77
Ministry of Works (MoW), 26
Mirrlees Blackstone, 129
model
    hydraulic, 13
    mathematical, 32
Mowlem, J., 129

National Electricity Grid, 136
Navigational Working Party, 61
Neptun, Hamburg, 118
Netherlands, 147
Neva, River, 147
north bank dry dock, 100
    damage to, 105
North Sea, 5, 146

Oceanographical and Meteorological
    Research Committee, 25, 41
Otter, Joe, 32
overspill, deliberate, 41, 69

panel, main control, 129
Paris, Matthew, 3
Parliamentary Committee, 90, 140
Parliamentary Secretary, 58
Peine pile, 106
Pepys, Samuel, 4
Peterken, L., 105
Petty, A., 89
pier 7, 103
pier roofs, 88, 103
pile cutting, 109
pilots, 61, 75
Plummer, D. (Lord Plummer), 90
police, 53, 54
Policy Committee, 58, 67
Pollution and Siltation Working Party, 62
Port Clarence, 111

Port of London, 21
Port of London Authority (PLA), 24, 27, 37,
    132, 145
power packs, 115
precautions against flooding, 52
Price, Alan, 27, 32
Price, J.T., 90
Pritchard and Peach Ltd, 78
probability of surge tides, 42, 60
progress letter, 67
Project Manager, 59, 78
protection, standard of, 27, 28
public inquiries, 148
Public Health Services Committee, 58
Public Information Branch, GLC, 66
Pugh, Dr, 61
pumping stations, 18

radar, 62
radio, 136
rainfall, 13
Rance, tidal power station, 149
Ray, A., 106
Rees, Capt., 61
Reeve, J., 102
reflected wave, 32
Regent Tar Works, 81
Rendel Palmer & Tritton, 32, 39, 64, 80
research engineer, 60
Research Models and Equipment Ltd, 85
retractable girder
    high level, 34, 39
    low level, 39
return period, 1000 year, 68
review negotiations, 1976, 101
Rhine, 11,
Richmond sluices, 103
Rijkswaterstaat, 33
rising sector gate, 81
river walls, raising, 28, 65, 130
Rossiter, Dr, 59, 67
Rotterdam, 33
Royal assent, 90
Royal Docks, 101, 120, 130
Royal Naval College, 79

Scheldt, River, 33
    Eastern, 71, 147
Schofield, Prof. A.N., 54
Scotland Yard, 134
Scrutton, H., 40, 71
Severn, River, 148
    bore, 67
    Estuary, 149
sewage, 20, 91
shaft support structure, 87, 114, 124
    handling rig, 125
shafts, main, 87
    manufacture, 125

Shallow, P., 69, 90
Sheffield, 111, 114
Shell Building, 20
shift and latch mechanism, 115
sill placing, 107
silt, 1, 7, 12
Sindall Construction Ltd, 128
sinkage
    due to extraction of water, 13
    of South East England, 10
    tectonic, 10
site supplemental agreement, 108
sites
    Crayfordness, 37, 91
    Dagenham Dock, 57
    Ford Works, 57
    Greenwich, 43
    Limehouse, 43
    Long Reach, 25, 27, 43, 57, 139, 145
    upper river, 44
    Woolwich, 47
Smith Ltd, 90
Snell, E., 90
Somerset House, 20
Southend, 18, 65, 68, 71, 130, 135
Sparrows, 125
Standard Conditions of Contract, 94
statutory check, 78
statutory level of river banks, 23, 68, 79
Steering Committee, 58
Stow (historian), 3
storage, 104, 117, 120
storm surge, 2, 13, 104
Storm Tide Warning Service, 134, 136
strain gauges, 86
strike, 103
    dock, 121
structural model tests, 85
subsoil investigation, 81
Sunderland Forge and Engineering Ltd, 129
surge forecast errors, 135
surge tides, 3, 13, 104
    genesis of, 14
    rise in levels of, 4, 42
Surrey Docks, 7, 62, 75
Suthons, Cmdr C.T., 42
swing bridge design, 34

Target Cost Contract, 102
Tarmac Ltd, 93
Tate & Lyle Ltd, 80
Tate Gallery, 20
Taylor, J., 90
Technical Panel, Thames, 17, 26, 144
Teddington, 23
Teddington Weir, 65
Tees, River, 111
Teflon, 127
telephone system, 20

tenders, contract, 3, 93
Thames, River, 1, 12, 16, 139
Thames Barrier Act, 90
Thames Conservancy, 24, 62
Thames Estuary, trumpet shape of, 7, 16
Thames Flood Act, 23, 57
Thames Flood Section, GLC, 79
Thames Technical Panel, 17, 26, 144
Thamesmead river wall, 92
Thanet sand, 82, 103
Thaxton, B., 89
Thompson, G., 64
Thorpe, R., 122
tidal power, 149
tide ranges, increase in estuary, 16
Tilbury, 130
    docks, 130
    landing stage, 91
Timber Research and Development
    Association (TRADA), 89
Tower Bridge, 44, 66, 75, 149
trade unions, 102
Treasury, 102, 146
Trinity House, 26, 61
tunnel, built in association with barrier,
    148
Turney, S., 58
twelve hour shifts, 95, 98
Tyne, River, 135
Tysons Ltd, 103

underground railway system, 17, 18, 53
undershot flow, 82, 136
underwater concrete, 95, 98, 103
uplift, 95, 103
upper river sites, 48, 71

Valuation Department, GLC, 61
Value Cost Contract, 102
Venice, 13, 147
Vickers Hydraulics Ltd, 115
Victoria and Albert Embankments, 79
VOEST, 124

wall, boundary, 128
warning system, 25, 52
Water Resources Board, 63
Water Pollution Research Laboratory
    (WPRL), 62
Waverley Committee, 24, 144
West India Docks, 140
Westminster, 3, 70
White, Sir Bruce, 32
White, Sir Bruce, Wolfe Barry and
    Partners, 32, 39, 64
Whitehall, 4
Whitehouse, C., 101

Wick, 135
Williams, H. and Co. Ltd, 129
Wilson, H., 90
Wimpey Laboratories, 84, 92
wind tunnel test, 89
Wisconsin Centrifugal Casting Inc., 127
Wolfe Barry, 32
Woolwich Dockyard, 81
Woolwich Ferry, 80
Woolwich Reach, 23, 47, 57, 71, 72, 73, 80,
    83, 91
Woolwich site, 7, 48, 72, 75, 80

Working Party
  Amenity, 64
  Civil Engineering, 64
  Groundwater effects, 63
  Navigation, 61
  Oceanographical and Meteorological, 59
  Pollution and Siltation, 62
Workshop, 128

Young, A., 80

Zuckerman, Sir Solly (Lord Zuckerman), 46

Davy McKee

Turns concepts into reality

Davy McKee's expertise in the precision machining and assembly of large complex units, together with their considerable experience in the project management of multi-discipline activities, made the Davy Cleveland Barrier Consortium the natural choice for involvement in the design and supply of operating machinery for the Thames Flood Barrier Prevention Project.

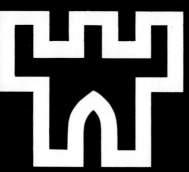

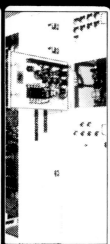

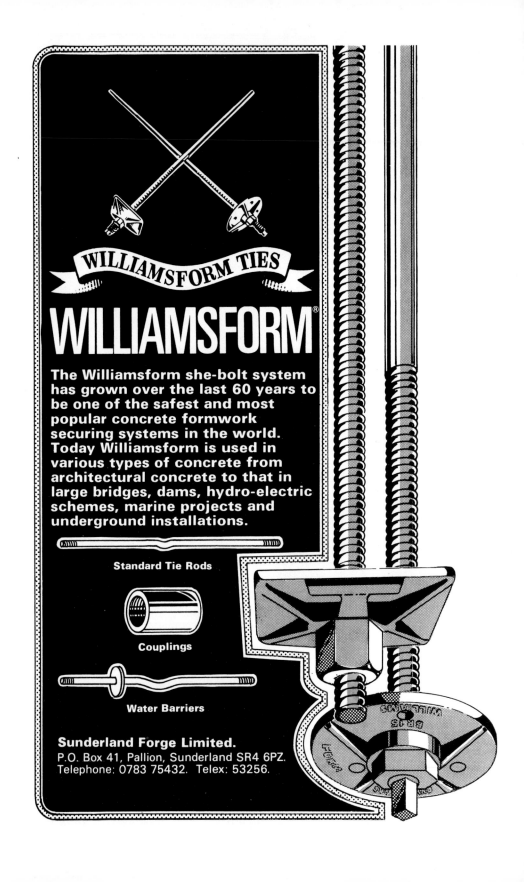

Shiers Diving

Underwater Engineering for
the Thames Barrier and on
major contracts throughout
the World

SHIERS DIVING CONTRACTS LTD

Head Office: 21 Millers Lane, Stanstead Abbotts, Ware, Herts SG12 8AF

Telephone: Ware (0920) 871151   Telex: 817765

The people who built the Thames Barrier.

The people who undertook the major civil engineering work on the Thames Barrier are: Costain Civil Engineering Ltd., Costain House, Nicholsons Walk, Maidenhead, Berks. Tarmac Construction Ltd., Construction House, Birch Street, Wolverhampton WV1 4HY. Hollandsche Beton Groep NV, 1, H.J. Nederhorststraat, 2801 SC Gouda, P.O. Box 63, 2800 AB Gouda, The Netherlands.

Heavy Lifting Expertise
Neptun cranes in action

Neptun was engaged for the installation of heavy lifts which demanded centimetre precision for the construc-tion of the Thames Barrier, built to protect London from the threat of catastrophic flooding.
The picture shows Neptun's selfpropelled floating sheerlegs HEBE 2 and HEBELIFT 3 lifting one of the gate arms into place. (24.5 m in diameter, 1.5 m thick, and weighing about 1,300 t.)

The Neptun Company has the know-how and the resources to take on great challenges – heavy lifts, difficult wreck removal jobs, complicated transports and demanding salvage operations.

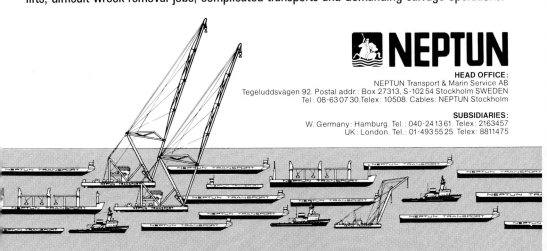

TYSONS

LIVERPOOL ENGLAND

Construction at its best.

When Quality & Reliability count-specify Mirrlees Blackstone Diesels

DIESEL ENGINES FROM 180 BHP TO 11680 BHP. GENERATING SETS FROM 120kW TO 8.25MW FOR BASE LOAD OR STANDBY DUTIES.

THREE BLACKSTONE
1500kW GENERATING SETS
PROTECT ELECTRICAL SUPPLIES
TO THE THAMES BARRIER

HAWKER SIDDELEY

MIRRLEES BLACKSTONE DIESELS

MIRRLEES BLACKSTONE (STAMFORD) LIMITED STAMFORD, LINCOLNSHIRE,
PE9 IUH ENGLAND. Tel: 0780 64641 Telex: 32234.

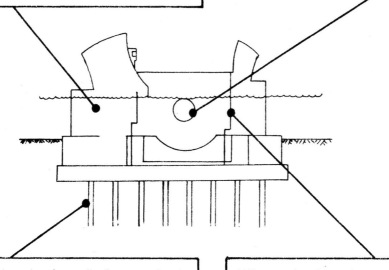

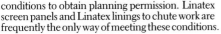
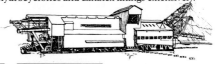

Balfour Kilpatrick and the Thames Barrier

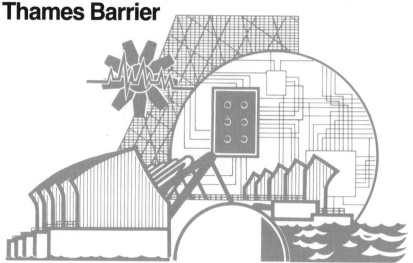

On the Thames Barrier Project behind the impressive civil and mechanical engineering of the piers and gates lie a complex array of power, cabling, control, alarm and firefighting systems, and a vast network of mechanical services which power, control and protect the Barrier. Balfour Kilpatrick are proud of their achievement in providing the vital concealed parts of the Thames Barrier Project.

Balfour Kilpatrick Limited, Special Projects Division, Glasgow Road, Deanside, Renfrew, PA4 8XZ.
Telephone: 041-886 4121. Telex: 779924

A BICC COMPANY

Benfleet Barrier.
For the Anglian Water Authority.
Engineer: Binnie & Partners.

Flood wall at Gravesend.
For the Southern Water Authority.
Director of Operations, S.W.A.

Permanent bank raising at Woolwich.
For the Greater London Council.

Thames Tidal Defences

Since the experimental river wall works at Stanford-le-Hope awarded
to the Company in 1973, Edmund Nuttall has undertaken fifteen contracts for
the Greater London Council, Anglian and Southern Water, and other Authorities responsible
for tidal defences on both banks of the river and the Thames Estuary.

Edmund Nuttall

Edmund Nuttall Limited 22 Grosvenor Gardens London SW1W 0DR.

INDEX TO ADVERTISERS

The Alexandra Towing Co Ltd A2
Andre Limited A17

Balfour Kilpatrick Limited A26
Benford Limited A8
Brentwood Communications Limited A28

Chubb Fire Security Limited A25
Claessen & Co Limited.. A27
Cleveland Redpath Engineering A5
Costain-Tarmac-HBM A9

Expanded Piling Co Limited A14

French Kier Construction Limited A16

GEC Distribution Switchgear Limited A23

Industramar Limited A4

Davy McKee (Sheffield) Limited A1
Milton Pipes Ltd A30
Mirrlees Blackstone A19

Neptun Transport & Marine Service AB A11
Edmund Nuttall Limited....................................... A31

Putzmeister Limited.. A24

Reinforcement Steel Services A15

Shiers Diving Contracts Limited A7
William Sindall plc A22
Sunderland Forge Limited .... A3 & A6

Tarmac Construction Limited A13
Terresearch Limited.. A20
Tysons plc.. A12

Watsons & Hillhouse (Plant Hire) Limited A18
West's Piling & Construction Co Limited A10
Wilkinson Rubber Linatex..................................... A21